DECISIONS MATTER

Ninety-Three Years of Experiences,
Surprises, and Joys
Beginning in Poverty on a Primitive
Pioneer Farm

Eleanor Maier
Share it

Eleanor Marie Maier

ISBN 978-1-68517-152-0 (paperback)
ISBN 978-1-68517-153-7 (digital)

Christian Faith Publishing
832 Park Avenue
Meadville, PA 16335
www.christianfaithpublishing.com

Printed in the United States of America

This work is dedicated to my husband, children, grandchildren, and our extended families, including church families for their kindness, support, and endless love.

I dedicate this also to my future great-grandchildren.

Contents

Foreword

My wife has asked me to write a foreword to her book. As I do so, I can hardly believe it is a reality. Only five months ago (February 2021), such a project was not on her or my radar screen. She had just had her aortic valve replaced in December 2020 and then had a pacemaker implanted in January 2021. Then she began the process of completing thirty cardiac rehabilitation therapy sessions. Prior to the aortic valve replacement, she had become so weak that she could hardly do anything for herself and sometimes felt too weak even to eat. This led to a visit to our family doctor's office and from there, immediately to the emergency room. Specialists decided that if there was any hope of her living much longer, she needed to have her aortic valve replaced.

For about six months while all the above had been happening, I had become pretty much the full-time care provider, back-rubber, and taxi driver to medical appointments and therapy sessions. While still very much in a recovery mode from the valve and pacemaker procedures, she received a call from two of her nieces asking her about what she remembered about some of her very early history. This got her dredging up what she could remember. As she was doing this, I encouraged her to make some notes. I thought all of this was only going to be about the very early part of her life. Somehow, how-ever, that suddenly morphed into a desire to write the full story of her remarkable journey—all ninety-two, now ninety-three years of it! It was going to be short, she assured me. That, too, changed!

No one has been more surprised than me that she decided to do this project at this stage in her life. As her strength returned, in the last four months, she has put an enormous amount of thought and work into this project. On the other hand, I am not surprised.

Once Eleanor decides that something is good and worthwhile that she wants to do or should do, she spares no effort to accomplish it. She is a remarkable woman. She is not without faults, but who is? She is a truly outstanding, capable, and an admiral individual. As you read her story, see if you don't agree.

When I was at the age when I began thinking about the kind of wife I would like to have, one day, an elderly woman walked down an aisle to a seat near me. I did not know her personally, but I had heard a lot of good things about her—how she was the lynchpin in her family and how she was generally admired throughout her rural community.

As I watched her walk down that aisle with such an air of kindly grace and self-assurance, I sensed in her such a possession of inner strength and wisdom that the thought struck me, "I would like to have a wife like her someday."

From that moment on, she became the ideal I was looking for in a wife. Well, God, in his wonderful gracious goodness and in his time, gave me just such a wife. That was almost sixty-six years ago. She, of course, is Eleanor.

At the school we were both attending, I spotted this gal in whom I sensed those same qualities which I had admired in that elderly lady. That set me off on a course in pursuit of Eleanor. It wasn't exactly easy. At that school at that time, the boys and girls were pretty much kept separate. I'm so grateful that God overruled and gave her to me anyway. I think that as you read about what she has meant and done for me, done for our children, and for others—very much for others—it is quite likely that you will wholeheartedly agree that she's a gem. I believe you will be blessed by her story, be fascinated by it, and helped by it.

May I provide just a little more detail as to why I say Eleanor and her story is remarkable? It is the story of a woman coming from a very limited background of great destitution, trauma, introversion, and somewhat of a "poor me" attitude who became a self-assured, basically content, happy, and fun-loving optimistic gal by the time I got to know her. This, even though she still basically had none of this world's goods as we say. In many ways, she was now focused on the needs of others. By then, she was already exhibiting some of the outstanding managerial and promotional capabilities she developed to deal with the sometimes very challenging, unanticipated situations she encountered throughout her long life.

What helped transform her into the "caring for others" kind of person she became is an intriguing part of her story. What that attitude led her to do and promote is another interesting part of the story. The courage this frequently took is remarkable, although she does not give herself the credit for that.

An intriguing part of the story is how she handled my departure from my faith into agnosticism for fifteen years. In a similar vein, how she handled her conviction that she should be home while her children were growing up, even though at the time, her earnings were very necessary to keep the family afloat. The spiritual welfare of others and ministering to their needs has become the passion of her life.

Eleanor's decision to write this story has sprung out of a desire to be helpful to others, even at her age of ninety-three. So far, both family and non-family members have been very positive about her story. So I recommend it to you too. I think you will also find much in it that is inspiring, surprising, intriguing, and worth considering.

Cliff Maier

Introduction

I am Eleanor Maier. May I introduce myself by noting the following things that have been true of me or of my life?

I was born into poverty but have retired in comfort.

I was born a first-generation immigrant in Canada but am a citizen of the United States.

I never graduated from high school but have a college degree.

I was raised as a devout Catholic but became a Protestant.

I was a secretary but chose to become a migrant worker.

I was born a girl but have often envied the freedom that boys have.

I have given a lot of time to making ends meet yet have always tried to put the interests of my family first.

How I coped when my Christian husband became an agnostic for fifteen years.

At one point, I was an ardent and successful businesswoman but then completely dropped out of the business world.

I am ninety-three years old but am still looking forward to what I might do next.

How did it all happen? What is the rest of the story? That is a question that I have been asked, in one way or another, many times over the years by members of my family, friends, one of my doctors, and even a professor. For example, when I was about sixty-five years old, I enrolled in a creative writing course at our local university. Our first assignment was to write an essay about our hometown.

In it, I wrote that there were no motorized vehicles—no cars, trucks, or powered machinery. There were no smoke stacks, no industry, or mills. On the main street of my town—the only street—one could see only horse-drawn vehicles of different kinds. In the summer, it was buggies and wagons of various types and sizes. In the winter, they were replaced with sleighs, cutters, and cabooses.

Caboose on a sleigh

The cutter was sort of a light open-boxed buggy-like contraption while the caboose was a little cabin on sleds. It was totally enclosed and was heated by a wood or coal-burning space heater.

Ann and I with our limousine caboose

At the end of the essay, the professor gave me a B- and wrote in red letters, "Please see me."

When the class was over, I cautiously walked to the front of the classroom and said, "You wanted to see me?"

To this, he responded rather firmly, "When I give you an assignment, I don't want you to copy it from a history book!"

I responded with a chuckle and a smile on my face, "I am older than you think. My dad was a pioneer farmer on some acreage in Northern Saskatchewan, Canada."

"Oh," he said, "then I will give you an A-."

I have chuckled over this incident many times since. After a couple of classes, my professor told me that I could ignore the regular class writing assignments and write more about my past experiences. This I did happily. Then, when the semester was over, he encouraged me to write the story of my life and added, "I will edit it for you."

I have often wondered since then if I should have taken him up on his offer at that time. That was thirty-five years ago, and he is now gone. Now at the age of ninety-three, I still often dream about experiences I've had in my past. Lately, I have felt more compelled than ever to actually sit down and write that story. Recent questions that my nieces, Judy and Marilyn Bader, have asked me about our past have caused me to dredge up once again what I can still remember. Now here I am, finally writing that story. My plan is for it to be a relatively brief account. I also intend to treat the early parts of my life more thoroughly. I will see how much energy I can still muster.

Regarding the sources from which I have drawn to help write this story, they are listed at the end of chapter 3. It will become evident to you why they are listed there.

I have appreciated very much the help my husband, Cliff, has given me with editing and the writing of this account and with sustaining me. I also thank both Keston Roberts, a young man presently living with us, and our son, Mark, for the very patient and great help they gave me with some computer issues. Mark especially spent hours helping me learn Google Docs and also with other computer challenges I have encountered. Larry, our son-in-law, spent many hours too with getting pictures ready to be inserted into the book. Both he and Mark helped to get the final product ready for the publisher. Our daughter, Fern, too has spent hours carefully reading and editing my work. I especially thank her, Susan Syria, and Judy Caldwell for their careful editing of the manuscript. Others who have read the manuscript and have given me some input are Mark and Tracey Maier, Jack Maier, Emma Maier, Judy and Marilyn Bader, Irma Powers, and my pastor, Brian Oberg. I thank all of them for their great help.

I have had a number of quite trying experiences in my lifetime but also many great ones. I trust that this story will be an encouragement, an inspiration, pleasure, and blessing to at least some who might read it. An important part of my life has been my faith. So I will include it quite naturally as it came into existence, developed, and affected part of my behavior. It's part of me. If I left it out, this would not be my story—at least not the honest one.

1

The Beginnings

My parents, Frank and Anna Koehl, once lived in Villach, Austria. That is on the southern and Italian side of the Austrian Alps.

Anna and Frank Koehl
My Mom and Dad

Villach is on the beautiful gently rolling foothills of those mountains. My mother's home was on a spacious green plateau of those foothills. The area was dotted with low-lying trees and was surrounded by a gorgeous view of the mountains in the distance. Nearby was the village of Villach. It had developed alongside a beautiful little mountain stream. I do not know just what the setting of my father's home was, but he was from the same general area.

In 1992, my husband and I visited Villach and the house that once was my mother's home. It had been renovated, but a section of the old home had been expertly preserved as part of the new structure. The whole place, including the yard and view, were just charming in 1992, and from all available reports, that had also been the case when my mom lived there in the early 1900s.

Dad, born in 1879, became a stonemason and never learned to read or write. Mom, born 1883, was a gracious lady, became a leading woman in her community, and was very active in her church. According to my sister Ann's recollections years later, Mom was involved in everything. Her church, out of appreciation, had her name engraved on a bell that it had hanging above it.

While still in Austria, Mom and Dad had six children. Tragically, they buried three of them there. One drowned in a nearby creek, one choked to death, and we do not know the cause of the death of the third one.

Mom had a sister whose maiden name was Marie Presinger. She had married a Mr. Wassertheurer who already had a son, Matthew. Marie became pregnant; but before the baby, Marcella, was born, her husband became ill and died from tuberculosis. At an earlier time, Marie's childhood sweetheart was a fellow named John Bader.

John learned through American agencies that America was "a land of opportunity"—a place where one could get rich. In 1908, he decided to leave Austria for that "promised land." He arrived in Minneapolis and, with few English language skills, was still able to get a job as a waiter in a large hotel.

Later, John learned that his childhood sweetheart, Marie, had become a widow. He contacted her and invited her to join him in Minneapolis. He told her that if she came, he would marry her. She accepted the proposal. She left her baby, Marcella, and her stepson, Matthew, with her mother, intending to return for them in a year. So, in 1910, she too sailed off to that "promised land." She and John were married shortly thereafter.

She got a job as a "cleaning lady" in an office building. She especially envied those ladies sitting at desks, typing while she "slaved away" as a cleaning lady. Significantly, and revealing some admirable farsightedness, Marie also took advantage of an opportunity to train to become a midwife.

Marie wrote such glowing reports back to Austria that Frank, my dad, decided to migrate to America too. The plan was that my dad would go there, establish a home for the family, and then they would join him in a year. Mom was left behind with their three toddlers: Tom, born in 1903, age five; Ann, born in 1907, age two; and Johnny, a new baby, born in 1908.

Mom with siblings Tom, Ann, and Johnnie
Grandpa and Grandma with Marcella and Matthew
(One year after Dad went to America)

When Dad got to Minneapolis, John and Marie invited him to bunk with them in their apartment. Dad, though a mason, was only able to get a job firing furnaces in a factory. He also changed his name from Frank Köchl to Frank Koehl because people had trouble pronouncing his German name. Apparently, the names of the rest of the family were changed too somewhere along the line, perhaps then.

While in Minneapolis, these three immigrants learned from a friend of another supposedly "great" opportunity. This time, it was up north in Saskatchewan. The promise was that they could get the title to a homestead, a whole quarter section of land—160 acres—if they cleared a relatively small amount of land in three years and lived on it for a certain length of time during that time. It sounded really good. They decided to take advantage of the opportunity.

Travelling by train, their plan was to claim and settle on some of this kind of land available in the Pig Lake District of Saskatchewan, roughly equidistant between Kelvington, Lintlaw, and Margo.

Dad's first shelter was a mere dugout he made into the side of a hill! He added poles and sod for more stability and warmth. Later, he built a log house. Ann said that the cracks in that log house were filled with cow manure or loam (that is mud made with a specific type of soil). Both of these materials stuck well when they were initially put into the cracks. Also, it did not dry out and fall out nearly as readily as some other types of materials that might have been used. It made sense to use that despite this seeming "madness." Many other pioneers did the same thing in their original houses. Cow manure ceased to have an odor after a short time!

Soon after their arrival in Saskatchewan, those three immigrants went to work clearing some of the trees from their land, and it was with axes. No chainsaws! One by one, they pulled the stumps with oxen or horses harnessed to a chain or rope tied to a stump. They cut up some of the trees they cleared from the land for firewood. The "breaking" of the land was done with a single-bladed plow. It is thought that initially he may have used oxen to plow his land. In time, Dad also was able to purchase a few cattle and a team of horses. These horses were the team he would later use to meet his wife.

The area had plenty of wildlife. Dad loved trapping and hunting. He became quite an accomplished trapper, especially of weasels, muskrats, and coyotes.

Being a mason, he was called on periodically to do that kind of work in the community. In fact, in 1913 and 1914 he, together with some others, laid the foundation and built the chimney for the only schoolhouse in the district. It became known as Heatherbank School. It was where my siblings and I would eventually attend.

When I consider the courage it must have taken back in about 1910 to set sail to a foreign land with very little in the way of resources and without being able to speak English, it is remarkable. For a man to leave an urban existence and venture into a wilderness devoid of modern conveniences—a land inhabited by wild animals and unknown, perhaps unfriendly people—I have to conclude that such a man, despite of his deficiencies, was in some ways quite an extraordinary man.

By 1914, Mom and the rest of our family were ready to join Dad in Canada. But then, they were delayed because of the commencement of the First World War. Once the war had ended in 1918, they were further delayed. Mom contracted that terrible Spanish flu that killed so many throughout the world at that time. She was sick with it or with the ramifications of it for two years. Marie's daughter, Marcela, had planned to rejoin her mom and travel to Canada with my mom and her three children. However, in 1922, Marcella decided not to continue to wait and left for Canada then. Courageously, she made the trip alone at only about fourteen years of age. Her half-brother, Matthew, on the other hand, chose not to migrate to Canada.

2

Mom Arrives

Finally, in November of 1923, after being separated from Dad for fifteen years, my mom and her three children, now teenagers, arrived in Invermay, Saskatchewan, after a long journey by steamboat and railroad. Invermay, in a still relatively undeveloped area of the province, was a hamlet with a couple of stores, a post office, a "Chinese" restaurant, and was about twelve miles from Dad's homestead, an even more undeveloped area. Dad met them with a heavy-duty farm wagon devoid of springs drawn by two maimed lean horses. Ann, my sister, later reminisced that one of them was blind and the other bowlegged!

Being November, it would have been cold. He probably had placed some heated stones in the wagon box and some blankets to keep the four of them warm. In Villach, the weather was rarely below freezing, and snowfall was rare. They probably were not dressed for the weather they encountered. Dad treated them to a meal in the Chinese restaurant. All in all, the new arrivals were not impressed with anything so far; and it got worse.

After the meal, they started on their journey to their new home. Tom, my brother, described the road as being no more than a trail that went through sloughs around bushes and over rocks and stumps. With a wagon like that, one felt every bump and every stone you hit. No doubt it was the roughest ride they had ever had in their lives.

Dad first stopped at Mom's sister Marie Bader's house. Marie served them chicken soup, which Ann said "tasted terrible." After the meal, Dad took Mom and the teens to their new home just a couple hundred yards from Bader's house. When Mom saw it, she started to cry and went back to Bader's house and slept there for the next two nights. She is said to have said that if she had the money, she would have turned right around and gone back home to Villach.

She had come from a middle-class environment and landed in raw primitive poverty. Mom never adjusted to it. She was a very unhappy woman. The log house was only fourteen feet wide and sixteen feet long. It had an upstairs and a built-on porch. The roof leaked some when it rained. And remember what the cracks were filled with? There was no bathroom, not even an outhouse. Mom insisted that Dad build one, pronto. The bit of furniture in the house was all made out of poles Dad had cut down.

The teens attempted to adapt. Tom worked on larger farms in the summer and fall, then came home and trapped during the winter. Eventually, he obtained a quarter section of land one mile south of Dad's land, married, and had eight children. They were Margaret, Marion, Gladys, Frank, Betty, Darlene, and Norman. One died as an infant. Tom was only sixty when he, too, died of a heart attack.

Ann was no happier on the farm than her mother. She said that in Austria, "We were never without or in want of anything. We had a happy-go-lucky childhood." She, too, had an especially hard time accepting what she found in Canada. After arriving in her new home, she went to Heatherbank School for two years, attempting to learn English. She then left for the city and did domestic work for five years.

Later, she worked in a beauty shop—in a sense, she did an apprenticeship there—and became a licensed hairdresser. Eventually, she had her own beauty shop. She married a German immigrant, Rudy Sydow, lived happily, had no children, and lived until she was 102 years old.

Johnny was only fifteen when they arrived in Canada. With him, Mom suffered another major blow. At the age of eighteen, he had an appendicitis attack and had surgery. He suffered some complications from it and died on the third day. He ate bread that third day after surgery. Some say that that was the cause of his death. This development meant that my poor mom had now suffered through seeing four of her children die.

I must not forget Marie's daughter, Marcella. She passed the eighth grade at Heatherbank and then went to business school in Saskatoon. She had a job with a collection agency, ran into some problems, and then she disappeared. No one had any idea of her whereabouts for almost one-hundred years. All kinds of things were speculated about what might have happened to her. Maybe she had been kidnapped, maybe murdered, etc. Given the environment she came from in Austria to what she found at her new home, it was also thought that perhaps she decided that she wanted to disassociate herself from her family and consequently deliberately planned her own disappearance.

In March of 2021, what happened to her was finally discovered. My niece and also Marie's granddaughter, Marilyn Bader, a history major in college, couldn't rest without continuing to try to discover what happened to Marcella. She searched everywhere—genealogical records, municipal records, newspapers, etc. She and a friend finally discovered her whereabouts.

Marcella is now gone, died at age eighty-three, and is buried about an hour from Marilyn's sister Judy's home on Vancouver Island, British Columbia. She had married Joseph Walcer. They had moved into the far north of Canada and had a trapping business there, then elsewhere, but still primarily in the fur business. They had one son, Walter. He had five children. Only two of them are still living. Marilyn has planned to meet with them this coming summer of 2021. In a conversation Marilyn had with Audrey, one of the surviving children, Audrey, said that her grandma never wanted to converse about her past.

From newspaper reports that Marilyn discovered, Marcella and her husband seemed to have been happily married as they engaged in various aspects of the fur-trading industry until their retirement on Vancouver Island. It is great that these facts regarding this story have been discovered and that it has such a gratifying ending to what was such a baffling mystery for years. Marilyn is to be congratulated for the great detective work she did.

3

Accommodating
a New Family

Mom always remained quite unhappy living in those primitive conditions. She gradually did seek to adjust and sought to make the best of her situation. Sometime in the next few years, Dad disposed of his original quarter section of land and acquired another one-half section and still adjacent but on the east side of her sister's home, the Baders. A new home was built on it.

The big attraction of this new piece of land was that Pig Lake was on it, and muskrats and ducks were plentiful. The lake was small, but it never dried up. Dad only cultivated about five acres of this new property. To protect his horses and cattle in the cold winter months, he also built a barn with a hayloft in it. His farm implements were minimal, basically a one-bottom plow, harrows, a hay mower, and a hay rake. Besides a few horses, he also had several cows and some pigs and chickens.

During this period of time, too, Mom and Dad began another family. First, one was born, then two, then three, then four, and, finally, five more children were born. The first one, Alfred, was born in August 1924, exactly nine months after Mom arrived! Then two years later, in August 1926, Otto came along. A year and a half later in June 1928, I was born. Frieda arrived eighteen months after that in December 1929. Then, Hansie, the final addition, made his entrance in June 1931. Mom was already forty-five years old when she gave birth to her last child, and fortunately, all of us were born healthy. Both brother, Tom, and sister, Ann, had left home by this time, so Mom had her hands full with five very young children.

Up to this part of this story, I have gleaned much of the information in it from histories written by my brother, Tom, my sister, Ann, and my niece, Gladys, as found in *A History of Lintlaw and District*, entitled *Echoes of the Past* and published around 1980 by the Lintlaw Historical Society in Lintlaw, Saskatchewan. Some of the information also comes from my recollections of conversations and notes I had written years ago after conversing with sister, Ann, and other members of the family. More recently, I have profited especially from research and conversations with my nieces, Judy and Marilyn Bader, my younger sister Frieda's children. Beyond that, most of the rest of the story is based on my own recollections; they are engraved indelibly on my mind and heart.

4

Life with Dad and Mom

You will recall that at one time, I took a creative writing class and wrote some essays about my past. Beginning now, I will be using some parts of one of those essays; however, I have reserved the right to make a few minor changes when that seems necessary. So here goes:

> My childhood years, by today's standards, were bleak; yet at the time, I didn't feel underprivileged or neglected. It was the way it was. We grew up in an isolated parkland away from all advanced civilization that might have caused us to feel deprived. Not only were we shut out from the rest of the world because of our location, but also because of our lack of access to any media. We had no radio or telephone, and never heard of television. Nor did any newspapers or magazines ever grace our home.
>
> Dad loved that pioneer life. He prided himself in providing for the family basically from the proceeds of his hunting and trapping. Our menu included a variety of meats—ducks, rabbits, partridge, and venison. He used to trap muskrats, coyotes, weasels, and some mink for their furs. I loved my Daddy and in my childish way helped him skin those animals—I used to like the smell

of weasels! Out of wood he whittled frames for the hides and hung them upstairs to dry. Once they were dried, he sold them in a town about ten miles from home and bought groceries. The groceries were basic—salt, pepper, flour, cereal, sugar, and coffee. I can remember what a treat it was when he sometimes brought home raisins or bananas.

Going to town was a day's work. Our vehicles consisted of horse-drawn contraptions. During the summer, he used an old chuck wagon which piggy-backed on an open box-like structure that provided space for passengers and whatever else needed hauling. During the winter months, an open-boxed sleigh replaced the chuck wagon; but dad placed heated rocks into the box to help keep the shivering passengers warm.

One summer day, when I was about six years old, another catastrophic blow occurred. As Dad and us kids were coming home on a hayrack, we saw our house in flames in the distance. It burned to the ground. We lost what little we had. No one was injured, but it left us homeless. The family, however, rallied around us and helped construct a new home in a very short time. In the meantime, we slept in the hayloft of our barn.

The new house was built with lumber but was only about twenty-by-twenty feet. It had two rooms on the main floor—a kitchen and living room—and a one-room second floor. One could stand upright only in the center of that room. The beds were placed end to end, no closets. The only furniture in the living room was a cot and a wooden chair. A pantry was also attached to the house. Dad built a rectangular table with stationary built-in benches on both sides of it. In addition to that, there was a woodburning cookstove, a wood box, some shelves for dishes, and a tent heater in the kitchen. The heater would turn red when it was fired up because the casing was so thin.

Our new house with siblings Ann, Otto, Me, Frieda, and Alfred

While this lifestyle seemed to be a delight to Dad, Mom never adapted to it. Their meager finances crushed any hope of any real change or of her ever returning to her homeland.

While "deprived," we kids still were able to enjoy various aspects of that free lifestyle. We enjoyed going on various nature hikes and especially going to Pig Lake about one-half mile from our house. The lake was shallow, so we just paddled in it. The boys loved using their slingshot. I can remember one time all five of us kids getting onto a horse and going for a ride. I was sitting at the back of the pack and was wearing a cap. On the way back home, it flew off. I cried out, "I lost my cap!"

Otto, sitting in front of me, just gave me a little shove, and off the back I slid! I didn't get hurt, but while the rest of them laughed, I was upset because they just rode off and let me walk home.

There were other reasons why I was not always a happy camper. My two older brothers were friends, and Frieda and my youngest brother, Hansie, were friends. I tended to be the loner in the middle and felt like it often. Sometimes they would be downright cruel to me. We talked about this when we were older, and they agreed about how unfair and cruel they were to me at times. They would pull my hair so hard that some of it came right out. I would cry. When our older sister, Ann, then a hairstylist, came to visit (though rarely), she would comment on how thin my hair was. I never tried to explain!

Our school, Heatherbank, was over a mile from home. It only held about thirty students. There was a big stove to heat it in the corner. Often, during the cold winter months, the building was not cozy until about noon. Dad made a toboggan drawn by a horse for us kids to ride on to go to school. In that below zero weather that we often experienced during the winter months, it just was too far to walk. Occasionally, the temperature would even drop as low as fifty below zero.

I loved school. I listened attentively. I loved my teacher, Miss Airey (she remained the teacher there for about five years). I even think I sort of became the teacher's pet in some ways because I was so attentive and such an eager beaver when it came to learning anything. I would catch on quickly. I would even memorize some poetry without it being a requirement.

Still, I was an introvert. I felt I was homely. My sister had such fine features compared to me. One of the reasons I felt so self-conscious was because we girls were not allowed to wear pants like some of the other girls, and in cold weather, the ridges of our long johns showed through our stockings, and that embarrassed both Frieda and me.

The two occasions that were special in our school lives were the Christmas concert and the picnic at the end of the school year. We often did plays, and the whole school always sang Christmas carols. I can remember one time when we were practicing carols for the concert, the teacher noticed that someone was singing out of tune. She listened carefully and discovered that the guilty singer was me. In front of the whole gang, she said to me, "Eleanor, please only move your lips." She really did want to be nice to me in that she allowed me to stand with the rest of the carolers. Once again, I felt crushed.

On a happier note, after the concert, Santa would give every boy and girl a gift and a bag of goodies. At home, Christmas would be celebrated around a big bowl of nuts and a bowl of hard candy. There was no gift exchange. At the end of the school year, there always was a picnic. There would be games, races, and the grand finale—home-made ice cream!

Jumping ahead a bit, our school had a softball team. We would occasionally go to a neighboring school, St. Eutrope, and play against them. Guess who the pitcher was? Yes, it was me! I would also play third base and was good at hitting the ball, although it often was a fly ball!

5

Dad's Sudden Death

Mom and Dad were continuing to eke out enough of an existence to be able to successfully raise their second family when another catastrophic blow struck. Dad became ill with dropsy (known in 2021 as congestive heart failure) and died suddenly on July 19, 1936. How would this depressed woman survive and provide for this young family in those primitive circumstances? I was only eight years old, my sister was six, and my brothers were four, ten, and twelve.

I can remember the day Dad died so well. He was scheduled to go to the hospital the next day. He had sent us kids out to fix a hole in the fence. When we returned, I hurriedly ran into the house, into the living room to tell Dad that the fence was fixed. What I found was alarming. Dad was lying there with his mouth and eyes wide open and his one arm draped down beside the bed. I said, "Mommy, Mommy, come and look at Daddy!"

She came, looked, and raised her arms above her head, and looking heavenward, said, "*Mein Gott, Mein Gott er ist starb* (My God, My God, he has died)." She immediately sent my brother, Alfred, to Auntie's house about three-quarters of a mile away to tell them. The news quickly spread.

Soon, a casket was brought to our house. There were no funeral homes in the area at this time. Dad was placed into the casket and left in our living room. It took up most of the space in the room and was left open. Not being embalmed in the heat of summer soon created problems. In a couple of days, a bucket was placed under the casket to catch fluids that were dripping from it.

Before they carried out the casket, Mom knocked on the casket five times. My aunt pulled her away (this was considered an act of love and respect for the deceased person but also carried with it superstition; each knock represented a year, and the one who did it would die of the same disease in the number years that they had knocked).

After the funeral, I remember asking a profound theological question. I asked Mom, "Where did Daddy go?"

She said, "To heaven."

6

The Summer after Dad Died

I don't remember any discussions about religion of any sort before Dad died. We had no Bible. The Catholic Church, at the time, taught that the laity was not allowed to read the Bible. Only the clergy could understand and interpret it. Attending the midnight mass on Christmas Eve was a must, though. Dad would heat stones on the cookstove during the day, and then put them into the open sleigh box. Mom had us put on the warmest clothing we had and loaded us into the sleigh box with blankets wrapped around us. There, huddled around the warm stones, we took the ten-mile journey to the Catholic Church in Lintlaw. The outing was an exciting experience for us kids; however, the mass was totally in Latin.

The summer Dad died, Mom sent us kids to catechism for a week also in the Catholic Church in Lintlaw. My twelve-year old brother, Alfred, hitched up a horse to a single-seated buggy we had at that time, and the five of us piled into it. I can remember Mom standing in the doorway and waving goodbye to us, I am sure with tears in her eyes.

I loved the experience. The priest really stressed teachings about heaven, hell, and purgatory. I can remember him teaching that a mortal sin would send us to hell, and a venial sin would send us to purgatory if our sin was not confessed to the priest. I became very interested and concerned about where I would go when I died. I thought and hoped I would at least make purgatory.

We were taught to say the rosary. To say the rosary, a person would repeat the Hail Mary prayer about ten times over and over and the Lord's Prayer in between. We also would include the Apostle's creed once or twice in the ritual. Saying these prayers, the priest told us, would mean that we laid up indulgences, and that would shorten our time in purgatory. Somehow, I got a rosary and began what I thought was my journey through purgatory. I can remember praying as I went to sleep.

That summer, too, Otto, my ten-year-old brother, had a serious accident, one more tragedy added to Mom's woes. He and Alfred were target practicing with the .22 by shooting at the sleigh that was in the yard. After Alfred shot, Otto ran to see if he hit the target. However, something backfired and hit one of his eyes. It was all bloodshot. He ran to the house and told Mom he fell and hurt his eye (he said years later that he never did tell her the truth).

This led to him having to go to the hospital in Yorkton, about forty miles away, to have his eye taken care of. Again, hard to believe, he was put on the train by himself to make the trip. Remember, he was only ten years old. The upshot of it all: his eye was removed and a glass eye inserted into the socket. It seemed like such a tragedy, but it all didn't bother Otto that much. It meant quite an extended stay in Yorkton. Otto was intrigued with the environment he experienced there, the city lights and all, so much so that he decided that he did not want to stay on the farm when he grew up. And he didn't. He adjusted well to operating with only one eye. Believe it or not, he became an operator of a heavy dozer, building roads on the edges of high steep cliffs in the rugged mountains of British Columbia.

The boys continued doing the chores, milking the cows, cleaning the barn, and hunting wild game for our next meal, etc. Our oldest brother, Tom, would come home and work the bit of cultivated land as it was needed. We girls helped, too, wherever we could, but we were only six and eight years old.

Mom did everything she possibly could to keep the family together. I can remember her knitting by the hour. She spun the wool with a treadle, a one-wheel spinning machine. The wool, coming directly from sheep, first needed to be carded. I did some of that too. Mom knitted our mittens, socks, and caps. I can remember seeing her knitting without looking at what she was doing as she was talking to us.

She also had a treadle sewing machine and sewed our dresses as well. Some of those dresses were made out of flour sacks. We purchased our flour in one-hundred-pound sacks. The dresses made out of that, no matter how serviceable and how good the seamstress was, they never looked very pretty! We often wore them to school because that was all we had.

7

Mom Gets Sick

After Dad's death, another catastrophic event occurred. Only six months after Dad died, Mom was also stricken with dropsy and became bedridden. We were so alone. Our nearest neighbors, our aunt and uncle, were almost a mile away. All of a sudden, we kids became the managers and doers of all the things that needed to be done to keep our family going.

Being the older of the girls and only eight years old, I became the chief cook and bottle washer as they used to say. My kid sister, Frieda, was a year and half younger, and I began to feel that she was Mom's favorite. It seemed like I had to do all the housework. I begrudged the fact that Mom didn't insist that Frieda help me with the dishes. Freida and I talked about this since then, and she agreed that it was unfair.

Speaking of washing dishes, one time, when I was doing the dishes, my brother, Tom, dropped by. As he noticed me doing the dishes, he scolded me for not doing a good enough job and said that I needed to be sure the dishes were clean. We would get sick if they weren't. I felt crushed. I was trying to do the best I could.

I can remember my two older brothers, Alfred and Otto, going out into the woods with their .22 rifle to get food for our dinner. Invariably, they would bring home a rabbit or partridges or a duck. It was my job to dress them. I don't recall being squeamish about having to do this as I would be now. I had watched Mom do it. I can remember skinning the rabbits and partridges. The ducks I'd pluck and singe off the tiny down feathers by holding them over a burning piece of paper on the stove!

Sometimes I would go out into the yard and catch a chicken, put its two legs together in one hand, lay its head against a log, and with an axe in the other hand, chop off its head. I can hardly believe I did this. Then to get the chicken ready for dinner, I would put the chicken into a pot of boiling water to make it easier to pluck its feathers. Of course, from her bed in the adjoining room, Mom told me what to do, step by step. I can't remember ever using a cookbook; I couldn't have read it anyway! I had only completed the first grade at the time.

The cooking instructions were to put in some flour and some milk, etc., never to use four cups of flour, and one cup of milk, for example. I used to take a spoonful of whatever I was cooking to Mom for her to taste and tell me what spices needed to be added. The only seasonings we had, however, were salt and pepper and sage for poultry dressing. My goulash turned out to be "pretty good!" It always got eaten!

Cream cans

Not only did we not have a cookbook, we didn't have running water, a fridge, or freezer. Dad had dug a well and cribbed it with planks and covered it with a wooden lid. We dipped the water out of it with a pail tied onto a rope. The well froze up in the winter. We then melted snow for our water supply. I can remember picking rabbit "turds" out of the snow before it melted! For a fridge, Dad had built a little hut about six-by-six feet. The guys would cut blocks of ice out of the slough behind our house, haul them into the hut, and then cover them with sawdust. This would keep the ice from melting for a good part of summer. Perishables would be stored in that hut.

In the summer, to keep the cream or milk cold, we would tie ropes onto the handle of a two and a half gallon or so cream can filled with either cream or milk and lower it down into the water in the well.

Of course, we cooked on a woodburning cookstove. There were no gauges to control the temperature either on the top of it or the oven. You just had to be careful to put only enough wood into it for it not to get too hot but hot enough. This was especially important when it came to baking. We used to bake eight loaves of bread at a time at least once a week. I can remember kneading that dough with my little hands. The bread turned out okay!

Electricity was nonexistent. The house was lit by a coal-oil lamp, and for the barn, we used a lantern. Both had a container at their base which was filled with coal oil, and both had a wick in them that was threaded upward through a cover. The wick was lit and was surrounded by a glass globe. These lights did not provide much light, but we considered them adequate since that was all that we knew.

The job I dreaded most, especially during the winter months, was doing the laundry. The first step was to melt enough snow to have water to do the washing. Our laundry equipment consisted of a big round tub, a washboard, and my hands. I scrubbed the boys' big heavy fleece-lined full-body underwear over and over on that rough washboard, then twisted them to wring out as much of the water as I could. I think they must have worn their clothes for a whole week without changing! That sounds absurd now, but they each only owned two pairs, and I washed only once during a week.

After washing them, Mom had me put them into an oblong-shaped copper boiler half full of water and boil them on the stove to help lift out any additional soil. I really can't fathom how that could have helped get any more of the dirt out of the clothes.

Our dryer was an outdoor clothesline! Regardless of the weather, the clothes had to be hung out! I especially hated hanging out clothes during cold freezing weather and then carrying those stiffened underwear "mannequins" back into the house and putting them over another line upstairs to finish the drying process.

Another job I loathed each week was scrubbing our bare wooden floor laden with the dirt that the five of us had tracked in from the yard. I had to get down on my knees and literally scrub off layers of dirt in places. I can remember being proud of that clean floor when I had finished, but it wasn't long until it needed to be done all over again.

8

A New Home

As the year passed, Mom's illness worsened. I believe that it was by the spring of the first year after my mom had become ill that our Aunt Marie and Uncle John Bader graciously took all six of us to their home to live with them. From this point forward, until Marie got her first grandchildren, I will be referring to her as Aunt or Auntie in this story. In actuality, we kids called her *Tontie* (German for Aunt).

Aunt Marie and Uncle John Bader

In many ways, Auntie was a very gracious lady. By her generosity and hospitality, she had endeared herself not only to her family but also to many in the community. She delivered most of the babies in the community, and many called her Ma Bader.

In 1919, when she thought that she was going to deliver another baby in the neighborhood about four miles from her place, they turned out to be twins! The mother, Mrs. Berggren, who had a very difficult delivery and already had four children, was rather distraught at having twins. One of the babies was not well either. You guessed it. My aunt offered to take the sickly one. The mother agreed. This baby was then adopted by the Baders and named Hans.

By the time Auntie took us into her home, Hans was already eighteen years old. In addition to Hans, she had also taken in two

Bader's house and car with Hans and Granny and us five kids
Frieda, Hansie, me, Alfred, and Otto

homeless boys. One was Ray Greensides who was fourteen when he was taken in. The other one was Harold Sunderlick who was mentally challenged. Harold came and went. Ray stayed with the Baders until he married at about age thirty. Now to that group, six more were added to Auntie's "family." Quite amazing!

The Baders' house, a modest two-story, was made out of lumber. It would have been no more than twenty-four or twenty-six feet wide. A one-story addition was added onto one side of it. There were two rooms upstairs. A bed filled one room. It did have a small closet and a free-standing toilet with a bucket that needed regular emptying. They still had an outhouse. An *Eaton's Catalogue* was used as toilet paper! In those days, this was rather common in rural communities. The other upstairs room had two beds, end to end. The stairway took up the other side of the room.

The downstairs consisted of three small rooms—a kitchen, dining room, and living room. The furniture was modest. There was a couch that folded out into a full-sized bed in the living room. It was sort of the guest bed. Uncle and Auntie slept in separate beds. Frieda slept on a cot beside Auntie's bed, and I slept with my aunt. Ray and Hans slept together. Harold slept with Uncle when he was there.

The Baders also had a bunkhouse about twenty-by-twenty feet square nearby. It only contained a heater and several cots. Mom was placed in a bed out there, and it was also where my brothers slept. During the day, it was my job to tend to Mom's needs.

Mom was repeatedly hospitalized in the next couple of years. I can remember one time when she was in the Kelvington Hospital, about twelve miles from home, I decided to visit her. I got on a bike and rode over rough dirt and often loose-graveled roads. It wasn't easy. I was probably eleven at the time. As I think of it now, I am also so very glad that I made that journey to visit her when she was so much in need of love and concern.

9

Mom's Final Days

During the last couple of years of my mom's life, she required more and more care and medical attention. Auntie finally decided that she had no choice but to put her into a government-supported nursing home. My mom called it "the poor house." And now that already broken woman became even sadder.

The home was in Whitewood, Saskatchewan, probably more than one hundred and fifty miles away. By this time, the Baders had a car. Twice, while Mom was in Whitewood, my aunt and Hans loaded us five kids into the car and took us to visit Mom. This was in the dust storm years, too, in Southern Saskatchewan where Whitewood was. I can remember encountering a dust storm that was so bad that we could not see and had to stop. When the wind died down, we discovered that we fortunately had stopped between telephone poles that were down on either side of us.

I can remember, too, how Mom wept when she saw us kids and how she cried, "*Oh, meine kinder, meine kinder* (Oh, my children, my children)." She looked so pathetic. Water was oozing out of open sores on her swollen legs, and her bloated stomach was stretched all out of shape.

Mom died on August 21, 1941. I was thirteen years old and now an orphan. There still were no funeral homes in the area. She was brought home from Whitewood in a casket and was put into the granary to await the funeral. My aunt insisted that us kids view Mom in the casket. She was only skin and bones. Her face was all bruised for some reason. When I saw her casket lowered into the ground, and some dirt thrown on it, I was heartbroken and cried in horror.

10

Life at Baders

It is interesting to note what a different environment we found at the Baders compared to our place. It was like moving from poverty to a middle-class situation. Their half section had been fully developed into farm and pasture land by 1940. They had modern farm equipment for those times, a tractor, a huge barn with a hayloft, a good number of cattle and pigs, pens for them, a chicken coop filled with chickens and turkeys, a huge garden, and a brand-new Ford car. The spacious yard was well developed and mowed. Water no longer needed to be hauled or snow melted to supply our needs. They had a well dug right under their kitchen with a pipe bringing water up to the sink where a pump was used to secure the water.

My aunt, also not always a well woman, suffered from a huge tumor in her abdomen. It had once been operated on, but the doctors felt that it was too dangerous to remove the whole thing. As a result, it continued to grow to where she looked like she was pregnant with triplets. She also had a mild heart condition and needed to take rests in the afternoon. Uncle John seemed to me to be a frail old man by this time and seemed to fade somewhat into the background as the younger men became more involved.

In managing operations, my aunt took the lead with her son, Hans, by her side. My older brothers pitched in and worked alongside Hans and Ray. The boys were ready to try and do everything that the older men did, sort of eager to "prove" themselves. And they got the jobs! My little brother, Hansie, tagged along.

Before we arrived at the Baders, they had a live-in maid. Perhaps for space reasons, she was let go when we arrived. I sometimes felt that we were now viewed as Auntie's hired hands. Frieda and I worked in the house, helping Auntie with everything that needed to be done—helping with cooking, cleaning, ironing, etc. We kids all worked pretty much all day.

We girls had a routine: Mondays was wash day; Tuesday, ironing; and Wednesday, mending. I don't remember what the designations for Thursday and Friday were; probably making bread one day, although we would make that as needed. Saturday was totally a workday. In the mornings, it was my job to clean the cupboard inside and out. I had to remove all the dishes and whatever else was in it every Saturday. I also scrubbed the floor of at least one of the rooms. I can remember wiping down the mop boards. One time, my aunt didn't feel it was done well enough. So she knelt down beside me, took my little ten-year-old hand, and showed me how to do it right. She didn't scold me, though. I remember feeling so hurt that she thought I wasn't doing a good job when I was trying so hard to do so.

Saturday afternoon, Frieda and I prepared food and goodies for Sunday. We made pan after pan of cookies and boiled and peeled lots of potatoes for potato salad. The reason for the Saturday rush was to prepare food for company that inevitably arrived on Sunday afternoons during the summer months.

The Baders always took Sundays off, except during harvest time. They only did necessary work, like taking care of the livestock, on Sundays. People came to the Baders on Sunday afternoons. They weren't specially invited; they just came. It just seemed to be the place where a good number of the neighbors came just to socialize and have a good time. My aunt loved to have company. Horses were tied here and there all over the yard. Usually, there were those who also stayed for supper. The Sunday evening meal was almost always potato salad made with home-made dressing, hard-boiled eggs, a variety of cookies, and sometimes home-made ice cream.

Although my aunt was a gracious lady—for me, at least—life still was not always a happy experience at her place. Even though Frieda and I generally were pretty great helpers, I think, my help was sometimes unappreciated! When I washed dishes, I often accidently dropped a dish, and it would break. My aunt invariably scolded me, hit me over the ear, and said, "*Du dummkopf* (*You dumb head* or *stupid*)!" Or she would call me, "Die, clumsy Eleanor."

One time, I remember carrying a whole pan of dishes that had just been washed from one spot to another. I dropped the whole works! Whew! I got the same treatment. I think part of the reason I had such trouble handling dishes was because I was so afraid of the consequences. I just hated being hit over the ear and being called stupid. I vowed I would never hit my kids over their ears.

My aunt taught us girls everything. For instance, she taught us how to sew, and I learned to sew dresses for her and us girls. Because Frieda was a year and a half younger than I, I caught on faster, and my aunt began to favor me on this score. I can remember feeling so sorry for Frieda once when Auntie was teaching her how to sew on a button. She threaded the needle and tied the knot on only one strand of the thread and began stitching. I said to her, "Why don't you tie the knot to include both ends of the thread? It will go twice as fast."

To this, my aunt responded to Frieda, "*Du dummkopf!*" I had heard this so often. That title was usually reserved for me.

Gardening was a big enterprise at the Baders. I think Auntie must have had an acre planted with just regular vegetables and that much again with potatoes. I can remember helping to plant the potatoes one spring day in May, and I had a splitting headache. I told Auntie about it, and she just lovingly said, "Poor child" in German and had me continue planting. Auntie and we girls weeded that big garden, and it often was hour after hour.

When wild berries such as saskatoons and raspberries became ripe, we picked them by the bucketful and then canned them. Some garden vegetables such as beans and peas were also canned in the fall. Even some meat would be canned. In the fall, Auntie would buy crates of peaches, pears, and plums; we ate some and canned quarts and quarts of them. You might ask, "Why was so much fruit canned?" Back then, it just was a tradition that a meal was not considered complete without a dessert. A serving of fruit met that need.

We also made sauerkraut. After shredding gobs of cabbage with a big mandolin, we put it into a wooden barrel. Then we would use a sort of wooden plunger to pound up and down on it until it was ready to be weighted down and eventually be ready to eat. Sister Ann told us that in Austria, she would be asked to stamp the cabbage with her bare feet! A similar process using a plunger turned cream into butter. All this involved we girls doing endless hours of work.

We girls not only helped with the household duties. We also helped in the fields. I coiled hay at times. At one point, I even graduated to raking hay with a hay rake, a machine that was about fourteen feet wide with rakes stretched between two large wheels and a seat in the center. It was pulled by two horses. I was rather delighted to do that. I felt "grown up." I was about twelve years old.

When it was time to harvest the grain crops, the boys would run the binder (initially pulled by horses, then by a tractor) which cut the grain, tied it into sheaves, and then tossed them out. Those sheaves then had to be set up by hand in tent-like fashion with the heads of the grain pointing upward. That was called stooking. This was so that the kernels in those heads of grain could complete their drying process before they were threshed. I was taught how to stook these sheaves, and I think most of us kids, if not all of us, were. I can remember how Auntie complimented me for the great job I did stooking and the speed with which I did it.

Threshing time with siblings

Threshing time was an especially exciting and social endeavor. Neighbor farmers would get together and go from one farm to another to thresh each farmer's crop. With horses pulling wagons with big hayracks on them, farmers would haul those sheaves to a stationary threshing machine. That machine would thresh the grain out of the sheaves and funnel it into granaries to be stored or into boxes on wheels to be hauled to market. The straw and chaff was blown out of the machine into big straw piles.

Threshing day(s) meant that there would be ten to twelve hungry men to feed. I can remember one day when Frieda and I were just twelve or fourteen years old, my auntie had to be away, and we were left to cook the evening meal for that gang. We did it. The men were so surprised and pleased that we two young kids had been able to cook and serve such a good meal for them, dessert and all!

Then we had the daily barnyard routine—feeding chickens, pigs and calves, and milking the cows. When we first came to the Baders, I didn't yet know how to milk a cow. I asked my aunt to let me try. She did, and I did a good job. Thereafter, guess what? I continued milking while I was on the farm. To milk a cow, we would sit on a little stool made out of a block of wood with a board nailed over the top of it. We would sit down beside the udder of a cow and start with each of our hands squeezing tits until all four got milked empty. Often, there was a kitty or two nearby, and we would love to squirt milk into their mouths, and they loved it too.

I had two pet cows. One was named May, and the other Queenie. When I would come into the corral to milk them, these two cows would come and stand behind each other next to me until I milked them. I loved those two cows—my two cows! I became responsible for milking seven of our cows each morning before I went to school at 8:00 a.m. and again each evening after suppertime.

In the evenings in the summer, there usually were a lot of mosquitoes around. Cows would swish their tails around to get some relief, and often, in the process, hit the milker, right in the face. We would build a fire, and after it was burning well, we'd almost totally cover it with dried cow manure (so cow manure was at a premium!).

That would create a lot of smoke and help keep the mosquitoes at bay, at least to some extent!

When we finished milking, we had to put the milk through a cream separator. It had a wheel and handle on it in order to turn the machine separating mechanism. The cream would come out of one spout and the skim milk out of another. The cream would be emptied into a large cream can and kept in a cool place to be taken to market. We also kept a lot of the cream with which to make butter. We always had an ample supply of butter. Taking the separator discs apart and washing them was an icky job, and it was my job too—another one I didn't like!

Generally speaking, Auntie didn't often let us girls be idle, even during downtimes. For example, she showed us how to crochet and do embroidery. We would happily embroider tea towels (often made out of flour sacks), pillow cases, dresser scarves, and the like. Both Frieda and I enjoyed doing this kind of work and did a lot of it. Auntie also tried to teach me how to knit, but I never took to that. It seemed too slow a process for me. I also liked to read when I could. I would do that by the light of a lantern in the evenings after the work was done. I remember reading *Anne of Green Gables* and relating to her. I felt like she got into similar tangles like I did.

I often felt that the boys were so much more privileged than us girls. We were never allowed to wear slacks, even when we were working out in the fields. The boys could be rough and tumble around, climb trees, and just be boys. They were never reprimanded for their behavior. Frieda and I, on the other hand, were reminded so often that we needed to be ladylike, even for the way we would sit. Playing like the boys was just not considered acceptable behavior for Frieda and me.

11

Making an Extremely Important Decision

Auntie was also concerned about our spiritual welfare. Like my mom, she also sent us to catechism in Lintlaw. Frieda and I (and maybe the boys too) were confirmed after that.

Me and Frieda confirmed

I remember so well one of the statements that was drilled into us by the priests at that time, and it was indelibly etched onto my mind. It was that "The Catholic Church is the one, the true, and the only universal apostolic Church."

Being confirmed meant we would have our first communion at that time too. It was all very meaningful and special to me. Auntie and some of the family had been going to church pretty regularly at this time. Each Sunday, before church, we would fast to prepare ourselves for our time of confession to the priest.

After being confirmed, I was still very concerned about where I would go when I died. I thought that if anyone could be sure of going to heaven, it would surely be a nun. So I decided that I wanted to become one. I told that to my aunt.

She responded rather disparagingly, "You're too much of a tomboy for that!"

That squelched that desire. At the same time, by this time, I had become a devout Catholic. I can remember arguing with a friend at school that the Catholic religion was the one and only true religion.

About 1942, a couple of individuals, Ramsey and Audrey Quark, came to our district and did what was called a Vacation Bible School at our school.

Pastor Ramsey Quark with Frieda and me on right

It was for all children above six years of age. My aunt sent all of us kids to it. She said that she had never learned anything bad in any church. I, however, soon detected that what this couple was teaching was quite different from what we had heard at the Catholic catechism classes. I began to wonder about what I had heard there.

The following year, that same couple returned. This time, however, it was not only to do another Daily Vacation Bible School but also to establish a church and to remain in our district quite permanently. They approached my aunt about renting our vacated house on our old farm. Auntie readily agreed that they could live there and there would be no charge.

It wasn't long before the Quarks decided to erect a little church about one-half a mile from the Baders. Some of us helped them build it. Here is a picture of Auntie and me spreading cement in the forms for the church's foundation.

Auntie and me helping Mr. Quark—build the foundation for our church

Ramsey Quark in the background is building more forms (incidentally, this church continued to exist there until around 2019). Soon, a number of individuals and families began attending, including all of us kids and Auntie.

Our little church

However, Auntie and we kids also continued to go to the Catholic Church and faithfully continued to go to confession and take communion. One day, after confessing my sins to the priest, he said to me, "Is there anything else?"

To which I said, "No."

He then sternly said to me that he had heard that we were going to a strange church near us. Then he said, "Don't you realize that that is worshipping a strange god? If you continue to attend it, I will no longer give you communion."

I was dumbfounded.

Frieda followed me, going in to confess her sins. He told her the same thing. We told Auntie what had happened. She became angry and later visited the priest about it. I don't know what he said to her, but when she returned, she told us, "I will never ask you to go to a Catholic church again!"

That was the end of going to the Catholic church for me, but I still had many unanswered questions.

My main questions centered on praying to Mary, the statutes, and purgatory. Pastor Quark was so wise. Although he had Catholics in his congregation, he never indicated or even hinted that some doctrine he preached from the Bible countered what the Catholics taught.

He just preached from the Bible, what the Bible said so that everyone was able to decide for themselves what the biblical truths were.

For instance, in talking about the teaching of praying to Mary, he simply expounded on verses in the Bible such as 1 Timothy 2:5 which states, "There is one Mediator between God and man, the Man Christ Jesus." This taught me that Jesus is our Mediator, not Mary. This was a major question for me.

In catechism, we had been taught that because Mary was Jesus's mother, she would have more influence with Jesus than we do; therefore, it only made sense to have her intercede on our behalf with Jesus, her Son. I used to feel so good to pray to the mother of Jesus.

When Pastor Quark taught about who we should pray to, he used passages in the Bible like Matthew 6:9–13 where Jesus told his disciples, "This is how you should pray: 'Our Father in heaven...'" As I listened to this, the question that arose in my mind was if we should pray to Mary rather than directly to God, even perhaps only at certain times, why didn't Jesus tell the disciples that at this opportune time?

With regard to images and if it was right to pray to them or to worship them, the pastor again taught what the Bible said, what God's guidelines were for this. For example, he taught what it said in the Ten Commandments in Exodus 20. There, in verses 3 and 4, it states with regard to images, "You shall have no other Gods before me. You shall not make for yourself an image in the form of anything in heaven above or on the earth beneath or in the waters below."

This I could clearly see was in conflict with the practice of us Catholics with the practice of having all kinds of images of both Mary and of Jesus which we were encouraged to adore, pray to, and even worship.

I loved the statues of Mary and Jesus. It helped me feel and understand the reality of them, but verses in the Bible like this clearly spoke against such a practice. Again, the pastor never mentioned the practices of the Catholic Church. He just taught the Scriptures and trusted that God would reveal the truth to us.

The issue of purgatory was the matter which concerned me the most. I had been so counting on that as an almost sure way of eventually making it to heaven. In Pastor Quark's teachings about how to get to heaven, he never mentioned purgatory. Again, he just taught what verses like Ephesians 2:8–9 had to say about what the basis is on which we get to heaven. He pointed out that those two verses say, "It is by grace you have been saved, through faith—and this is not from yourselves, it is the gift of God—not by works, so that no one can boast."

These two verses alone made it clear to me that we cannot work to earn our salvation (either while in a purgatory or to earn merits to get out of purgatory more quickly) and showed that our good deeds don't count so far as getting us into heaven is concerned. It says salvation is offered to us as a free gift. One is not required to work to receive a gift, but the gift offered to us has to be accepted to do us any good.

Wow! These things were so comforting and freeing to me. I didn't have to worry about earning my way. Jesus had already done that for me. Mr. Quark also often quoted John 3:16, "For God so loved the world that he gave his one and only Son, that whoever believes in him shall not perish but have eternal life." My daughter told me that this is the verse she most relied on in her college years. This teaching also has had a huge impact on her.

In some personal conversations with Mr. Quark regarding purgatory, he told me that the existence of such a place as purgatory cannot be found in the Bible. That was a shocker to me too. I have since learned that the idea of purgatory is an idea that was introduced into church doctrine by Pope Gregory in the twelfth century. This was long after the divinely inspired writing of the Bible had been declared complete. The last chapter of the Bible affirms that nothing is to be added to it too. It also declares that there are severe consequences for anyone who adds anything to the Scriptures.

Pastor also taught us that it is really an insult to God to try to earn our own way to heaven. What doing that effectively says to Jesus is, "You didn't complete the job well enough or do it well enough through taking on the punishment for man's sins on the cross." When Jesus said on the cross, "It is finished," he really was misleading people.

When I realized this, it reminded me of the time I was cleaning the mop boards, and Auntie took my little hand and did it over again. How crushed I was that she thought I didn't do a good enough job.

Quarks taught us many more things in the Bible. Especially intriguing for me were his sermons regarding what the Bible says about "the end-times." One night thereafter, there was a terrible storm. Stars were falling everywhere and swiftly darting across the skies and toward the ground—a meteor shower. The whole family rushed outside and gazed upward into the sky. I became very frightened. I thought the world was coming to an end. I dashed back into the house, fell on my knees, and began praying. I pleaded with God to save me. I told him that I believed in him. I asked him to forgive my sins as I had heard Pastor Quark say the Bible says we must do to go to heaven.

Looking back on it all now, I believe it was that night that I truly put my faith in Jesus and what he had done to save me. I accepted him. I accepted his gift for me. I believed—I mean, I really trusted what the Bible said about what he said he would do he would do for me! I believed that according to what the Bible taught, I became a Christian that night. A verse that helped me have assurance of that is found in John 3:36 which says, "Whoever believes in the Son has eternal life, but whoever rejects the Son will not see life, for God's wrath [still] remains on him." Also, I noticed that this statement used the present tense—has eternal life. It gave me that confidence that I had longed for earlier that I would be going to heaven when I died, not probably to purgatory.

In time, the Quarks invited two sisters, Vivian and Gertrude Strickert, to come and do another Vacation Bible School for the children in our district. They were great singers and loved the Lord Jesus so much. I was so drawn to Vivian especially. They had been students at a Bible School. I wanted to be like Vivian. Just from observing her, I began to desire to go to Bible school too. I was sixteen at that time. Vivian and I exchanged letters during the next few years. Later in life, we began sending each other our Christmas letters—something we still do to this day—for over seventy years. It was this relationship that caused me to make some important decisions later in life which I will share later.

Many times, I have been amazed when wondering why the Quarks chose to come to our rural district out in the middle of nowhere, so to speak. We were ten miles from three different towns—Lintlaw, Invermay, and Margo. They all had relatively sizable populations for that region of the province, unlike our Heatherbank district. Furthermore, the Quarks did not have a car or even bicycles. That is hard to believe but true. In our district, the houses were one, two, or even four miles apart. It made no sense from a natural point of view, but from God's view, it did. I believe the Quarks were tuned in to his directions. God knew that there were some people in that district who would respond to his love and would come to hear the Quarks teach the Word of God.

I can only say I thank God for having guided the Quarks to our district. I know that their coming changed both my eternal destiny as well as the direction of my life. I believe that this was not only true for me but for a good number of others too. Only heaven will reveal the results of their great work in that district alone.

I know it was very meaningful to my sister, Frieda, too. She went to church all of her life and took her children to Sunday school and church too. My aunt loved it. One of my brother Tom's daughters, Marion, who initially also began as a Catholic, attended Quark's church. Eventually, she married a Protestant minister. I suspect that the grounding and training she received through the Quark's teaching prepared her for that man and that role. I know of several others from our district whose lives were also transformed by God through their ministry.

12

Furthering My Education

Though we kids had to work hard, Auntie never let us miss school. She considered grade eight to be adequate for the boys. When they had finished that grade and were sixteen years old, both Alfred and Otto were sent off to find jobs working for larger farmers. Hansie, my youngest brother, now in his teens, remained with the Baders and became one of the main helpers in getting the fieldwork done.

It was different for Frieda and me. I think my aunt's experience of working as a cleaning lady in Minneapolis while the other young women sat neatly dressed at typewriters made her desire something better for us. She said that she didn't want us to become cleaning ladies. We both finished grade eight at Heatherbank. I took grades nine and ten in that same crowded one-room school. There was just one teacher for all ten grades which meant that I was tutored just a little.

When I finished grade eight, my aunt surprised me by purchasing a typewriter for me. She also enrolled me in two correspondence classes—shorthand and typing. I had never seen a typewriter before. When it arrived, she gave it to me, and I immediately tried to insert a paper into it to try it out. I attempted to do that by putting the paper under the keys! She laughed and told me where it needed to be inserted.

I loved learning. My aunt never had to tell me to do my homework, if I ever had any, nor to do the assignments for those correspondence courses. The only instructions I remember receiving from her on this score was, "You can't look at the keys when learning to type." Excellent instructions they were. By the end of the tenth grade, I was able to type about fifty words a minute and do about sixty words a minute in shorthand. What was next?

In 1945, I was sent to Saskatoon to take my grade eleven and stay with a couple my aunt knew. Some evenings, the lady of the house had meetings elsewhere while I was left at home alone with her husband. Sadly, he made sexual advances when she was gone. They had a couch and a chair in the living room. He would invite me to join him there. He would quickly take the chair so that I would have to sit on the couch. After being seated, he came and sat beside me and then put his arm around me.

Even though I was a rather shy, quiet, naïve country girl, I knew that this spelled trouble. I wrote home and told my family what was happening. I hadn't fully unpacked yet. They wrote back to tell me that they would send me a telegram saying that my aunt was ill and needed me to return home. I got the telegram and was greatly relieved to get out of that situation before something worse happened.

The Quarks heard about Auntie's dilemma. They suggested that my folks send me to take grade eleven at the high school at the Prairie Bible Institute in Alberta. They did. As I think of this, it is so amazing that the Baders would be willing to spend the money to do this for me and at this kind of a school.

Interestingly, Auntie had no problem with the regulations the school had. For instance, it had strict dress rules. No slacks. That wasn't a problem because Auntie didn't allow us girls to wear pants anyway. Dresses had to be well below the knee and sleeves below the elbow. I could sew and quickly got my clothes in compliance. The time came to leave, and I was put onto the train. Off I went to Three Hills, Alberta, for nine months. That was during the 1945–46 school year. I was seventeen years old.

I loved the school and the routine. I took advanced shorthand and typing classes as well as bookkeeping in addition to the regular classes necessary to complete the grade. All students were required to attend daily chapel and Sunday services. We were also encouraged to read a bit from the Bible every day and spend some time praying. Rules were strict. The boys and girls were housed in separate dorms and not allowed to socialize. Dancing, going to movies, and wearing make-up all were no-nos. I had never done any of this, so that was no challenge for me, but it did have an impact on me.

The teaching we received in the services were so like what the Quarks taught. There was a heavy emphasis on Jesus's last command given in Matthew 28:19 and 20 to go and tell and make disciples. They encouraged us to be witnesses and to share the good news of the Gospel with others. All this encouraged me to include some of what I learned when I wrote home. I think I became somewhat of an evangelist in my own way.

I completed the grade with flying colors and returned home. I didn't keep what I had learned from the Bible to myself. I was concerned that everyone would accept Jesus's pardon and be ready to go to heaven. I tried to share it, but it wasn't always accepted well.

13

My First Job

Before the summer of 1946 was over, my aunt decided to send me to another acquaintance, this time the Nixons in Regina. She gave me $100 and put it into a money belt for me. You know, I don't remember ever spending that $100. I wonder if it is still in that money belt somewhere! As she said goodbye, I remember her crying and saying, "I am losing my right-hand man." This time, it was for me to find my first job. It didn't take long, and I was hired as a clerk at the large Simpsons mail-order company. I liked my job but wasn't crazy about it because a lot of it involved just filing stuff away. But my aunt's dream for me had come to fruition!

I can remember the manager having difficulty with packing slips and invoices getting mixed up. Awards were offered for good suggestions to improve operations. I suggested that they use a different color for each of the documents. Wow! I was awarded $10 for the suggestion. That was a half a week of wages. I was pretty proud of myself. My pay was a meager $19 a week.

I also decided to take an advanced accounting class at night school. I walked back and forth, about a half an hour walk. One night, as I was returning home, a guy was on the other side of a wide street and was somewhat further behind me, and he was pointing to his crotch! I began to run as did he also. Fortunately, I outran him and arrived home, exhausted. When Mrs. Nixon saw me, she said, "You are white, Eleanor." I told her the story. I did continue, however, walking to night school.

The Nixons were devoted Christians and invited me to go to church with them. I met Margaret Anderson there, and we became good friends. Toward the spring of that first year, Margaret and I learned of a great opportunity in British Columbia! It was picking various types of fruit and being paid piecemeal by the pound. There was also a special on. One could take the train all the way from Regina to British Columbia for just $5. I still wanted to go to Bible school. I thought that was a long way off with the wages I was receiving. *What fun*, we thought. So we took off!

My aunt, when she learned of it, was, I think the word would be *furious*. How could I leave an office job to become a migrant worker? A mere fruit-picker? And I didn't even consult with her!! Wow—such brass!

14

A Migrant Worker

We arrived in Surrey, British Columbia, and found a large raspberry farm. The owner put us up in a little shack in the field! We picked hour after hour in the hot sun. The pounds added up. I was especially fast at picking and did very well. I was happy.

I was accumulating money to pay for Bible School. So in the middle of that raspberry patch, I sat down and mailed an application letter off to the Two Rivers Bible Institute at Carlea, Saskatchewan. That was the school that the Quarks had recommended. In a couple of weeks, the answer came. I was accepted. I was very happy, but would my aunt be? You guessed it. A big no!

I now had become a big disappointment to her twice. I had abandoned my job as secretary and resorted to being a seasonal worker. I regretted greatly that I had disappointed her so badly. Still, I felt it was the right choice for me. It changed my life in many satisfying ways. Because of it, my life became more rewarding and fulfilling than it ever would have been pursuing a career as a secretary. This, even though a career as a secretary, of course, for some can be just as worthy, necessary, and honorable as any other, and is an essential line of work. Furthermore, the skill of typing has served me very well personally. So to this day, in spite of her disappointment then, I thank my aunt for getting me started on learning this important skill.

While I was working in the raspberry patch, I noticed that my throat was swollen and went to the doctor. He diagnosed it to be a goiter. My mom also had a sizable one. I prayed and asked God to heal me from it. The goiter disappeared. Thank you, Jesus.

When the raspberry season was over, we decided to do a bit of sightseeing. We two brave (or foolish?) girls set out hitchhiking from one beautiful spot to another. It was exciting. We would only accept a ride if there was only one person in the car.

After this, we took the train to Kamloops to work in a tomato factory. We worked there for two weeks and quit. We didn't like it. Then we set out for Kelowna for a huge apple orchard there. We strapped on an apple-picking bag and went to work. A guy moved the ladder for us each time we finished picking the apples off the branches around us. I was making super progress. But then the manager came to me and said that I was grabbing the apples too hard and bruising them. He had to tell me twice!

Apple picking season would be over soon, just about the time Bible School was to begin. I said goodbye to my friend, Margaret, and hopped onto a train heading for the Bible School at Carlea, Saskatchewan. I was happy as a lark. On my way to the school, I could have made a detour and stopped at home for a visit, but I decided against it. I knew Auntie was quite unhappy with me.

15

My Initial Years at Two Rivers

When I arrived at the train station in Carlea, I found that it was just a one-store town. Folks from the school were there to pick me up. We travelled about two miles over a dirt road to that place known then as the Two Rivers Bible Institute (TRBI) or Two Rivers, the place I had applied to in that raspberry patch in British Columbia. Today, the Institute is called Nipawin Bible College and has relocated to Nipawin, Saskatchewan.

I was warmly received and immediately felt welcome. The matron, the supervisor of women, assigned a room to me. It was right next to hers. Most students had roommates, and the one assigned to be mine was Vivian Albertson (another Vivian!). We hit it off together immediately and chose to remain roommates for the whole four years of our time in Bible School. We still keep in touch to this day.

The accommodations were somewhat similar to what I left on the farm—no bathrooms or running water in the rooms. At the end of the hall, there were toilets with buckets that needed regular emptying. A generator provided electric lights. The coal oil lamps were obsolete and gone. Hot water radiators heated our rooms. The room was a comfortable size, probably fifteen-by-fifteen feet with a closet. Each room had a bed, a table, and a stand with a wash basin and pitcher on top of it.

Two Rivers was a sister school to the Prairie Bible Institute (PBI) where I had completed my eleventh grade. Most of the teachers were graduates of the PBI. Rules and the dress codes were similar, and the routine was pretty much the same.

The curriculum covered at least some study of every one of the sixty-six books in the Bible. It also included other classes such as English, church history, evangelism, and so on. Our classes almost always included heavy assignments. Vivian and I struggled with some of them. We would often get down on our knees beside our bed to complete them. In all, we both loved studying and learning more of what was in the Bible. My husband, Clifford Maier, and I wrote a detailed historical account of that school, so I will not repeat much of that here. The two-volume book, *A Journey of Faith*, has 700 pages.

The school would close for Christmas and New Year's. Students would usually go home for those holidays. I, however, cringed at the thought of going home after having disappointed my aunt so much. I had also experienced some rejection earlier after I returned from PBI when I would talk about my increasingly firm belief that folks needed to be sure of going to heaven and that it did not happen without making some decisions. Yet, in spite of my reluctance, I still felt compelled to go home, remembering that the Fifth Commandment asks us to honor our parents. Though my aunt was not a biological parent, she certainly had treated me as her child when I was in dire need.

My fears were realized. When I got home, I was treated very coolly, even harshly. I can remember one of those times when I was home for Christmas. Just before I was about to return to school, I got the mumps. The swelling went from my throat down into my chest. I hid the swelling and returned to the institute in that condition in bitter cold weather because I didn't want to remain in that environment any longer.

As at most educational institutions, different faculty and staff would visit various parts of the country to interest young people to come to Bible School. Mr. Wannop, the principal and head of the school, had created a trio for this purpose. The trio included Mr. and Mrs. Wannop. So rather cautiously, I invited that trio to visit my home district. When my aunt, being the hospitable woman that she was, heard of this, she invited them to stay at her place overnight. I went home to be there when they were there too. While there, Auntie continuously treated me very condescendingly in their presence. If I did something one way, she would scold me in front of them, telling me to do it another way. For example, I made the bed the two of us slept in shortly after we got up. She reprimanded me for not letting it air out. If I wouldn't have made it, she would have scolded me for not doing so.

I wanted to begin to live my life according to the outlook and values that I was learning. I believed that the Bible was our guide book. We were accountable to God and should seek to please and obey him. I felt I was honoring him and showing appropriate respect in giving part of my youth to studying what I considered by now to be his "instruction manual." A portion of Scripture that encouraged me along this line is one found in Matthew 5:11–12. God is pleased when we follow him.

16

Financial Realities and Surprises during My TRBI Years

When I look back on how I got by financially during my eight years spent at TRBI, first as a student and then as a staff member, I am amazed. The last cash I was paid for work done between 1947 and 1955 was in that apple orchard in Kelowna, British Columbia, as a "migrant worker!"

At TRBI, in order to reduce costs for both the school and the students, students were assigned two hours of gratis work daily. There were all kinds of jobs: cleaning, helping prepare food, doing some of the cooking, washing, ironing, farm and yard work, etc. The matron heard me typing in my room and so assigned me to help with the office work. So after all the disappointment and despite everything, one of my aunt's dreams for me was on the way to being realized even there at TRBI.

Every spring after the school year was over, the institute asked a good number of students to stay to work for the school for the summer. Doing this meant that their board and room costs for the next school year would be covered (no tuition was charged to any students, regardless). As you would probably guess, I was asked to be an assistant in the office and did this every summer thereafter while I was in school. This system also essentially meant that we had no money for incidentals or anything else. Often, I didn't have enough money even for a postage stamp. I would pray about my needs, and God would wonderfully provide, often in very surprising ways.

As I write this, I am thankful that Auntie had allowed me to keep that little typewriter she had given me when I completed eighth grade. I had tugged it all over British Columbia in my big heavy clumsy wooden suitcase. It was so great to still have it. It became my ticket to my "secretary" job at the institute, to doing neat class assignments, and eventually, it would become a reason why I became the institute's typing instructor. What a little treasure.

Every once in a while, an envelope with a twenty-dollar bill would appear under my door. I think it was the Wannops who did that. One time, my winter coat was getting quite worn down the front. One evening, I prayed and asked God to supply a new one for the coming winter. Summer workers took turns in making breakfast. The morning after my prayer, making breakfast happened to be my turn. One of the staff members who was in charge of farming operations at the school just happened to be in the kitchen that morning after I had prayed. He called me aside and asked, "Eleanor, do you need anything in the way of clothing?" I told him about my coat and my prayer the night before.

He responded, "This morning, when I was having my devotions, God spoke to me about asking you about whether you needed anything in the way of clothing. Make out an order for a coat and give it to me."

I was amazed and soon gave him the order. In a couple of weeks, my coat arrived. It fit perfectly. This is one of the most remarkable and immediate answers to prayers I had ever experienced.

One day, I was surprised to receive a letter from home with $100 in it. *Wow*, I thought. One thing I had really wanted and needed was a more serviceable suitcase. When I received that money, I planned to buy one with it.

My dad and mom had not left a will. So their land had to be left unpossessed until the youngest of us five children reached the age of twenty-one. When that time was up, my brother, Alfred, wanted to own the land and was willing to pay the back taxes to get it. He also needed all of his siblings to sign off on it. He called me and asked if

I would accept $100 to liquidate my share of the claim to the land to help facilitate the completion of the transaction. I agreed. I had never expected anything. One-hundred dollars sounded good to me! I was pleased and surprised when the money actually came.

To my astonishment and shock, one of my relatives sent me a blistering letter stating how selfish and thoughtless I had been to have accepted the money and to not have given it to my youngest brother, Hansie, who by now was married, had young children, and was struggling. I wasn't even aware of his financial situation. Little did this relative realize that I really was very much in need of money too. Although I was crushed and somewhat angered by the rebuke, I sent the money back to that relative. When Mr. Wannop heard about the episode, he purchased a suitcase for me.

To complete this story, a couple of years later, Alfred visited me at the school. He said he felt badly about what had happened. To my surprise, he gave me $50. That was a sacrifice for him too; he was still struggling financially also.

The Bible says that God will provide for our needs. I certainly experienced that many times during those Bible school years. The above are just a few examples of the sometimes totally unexpected ways he did that.

17

A Monumental Revelation

I thoroughly enjoyed my time in Bible School. The teachers were all so accepting and warm. As for students, it was one big happy family. We made friendships that have lasted over the years.

The Bible classes were inspiring. I enjoyed studying the Old Testament. I was surprised how the children of Israel repeatedly forsook the Lord and went after other gods and how they were severely punished for doing so. It made me wonder if that is how God viewed what I did when I so loved Mary and prayed to her to get to him.

A class that especially stood out for me was focused on the book of Romans. It was in that class that it dawned on me more fully for the first time how wonderful a pardon Jesus had accomplished on the cross for me. I stood before him completely sin-free and would not be barred from entering into heaven. My sins were forgiven *and* forgotten. Forever! I would never be under any condemnation for my sin before God. That was a monumental revelation for me, all because I had come to believe in Jesus and had personally accepted his pardon. Two verses that still stand out for me to this day and that teach that are the first verses in Romans in both chapters 5 and 8.

The school had a heavy emphasis on obeying the last commission of Jesus regarding going into all the world to preach the Gospel, to baptize, and teach. Quite a number of students felt the call of God to go to some foreign field to be a missionary. I, however, never felt such a specific call. Some of my best friends did. One was Helen Peters. She went to Zambia, Africa, as a single woman and served there for many years. Now retired, we still keep in touch; and each time we have visited her area in Canada, we have visited her too.

When I studied more about being baptized, I began to feel that I needed to be baptized as a believer. I had been baptized as an infant, but I discovered that is not what the Bible taught. When children were brought to Jesus, he blessed them. He did not baptize them. In the book of Acts, it stated, "Believe and be baptized." An infant can't believe. Also, as a Catholic, I was taught that baptism takes away our original sin. However, the Bible clearly teaches that it is Jesus's blood that takes away our sin as a quick glance at Hebrews chapter 9, verses 12–15, clearly shows. As the old hymn clearly says:

> What can wash away my sin?
> Nothing but the blood of Jesus.
> What can make me whole again?
> Nothing but the blood of Jesus.

Therefore, when the opportunity came, I was baptized in the Carrot River along with others. Interestingly, Cliff was baptized at the same time. At that time, we hardly noticed each other.

The junior year of Bible school was an especially fun one. A tradition had developed that students in their junior year would plan and present a special program that would be a challenge to the graduating seniors. During the planning, the guys and gals were allowed to work together, which was a rare occurrence. The juniors presented their challenge to the seniors during a very special evening preceded by a delicious dinner.

The seniors, at their graduation event, would present little talks enlarging on a specific topic. For my senior year, four seniors out of our class of twelve were selected to speak. I was one of them! I can remember that my topic was love. I recall that the scripture passage that I used was 1 Corinthians chapter 13, a great chapter on love. It focuses on the importance of love in life. When Jesus was asked what the greatest commandment was, he said, and I paraphrase, "to love God with our whole being, and to love our neighbor as ourselves." Where it is not present, our words are like meaningless sounds, like sounding gongs or clanging cymbals. The driving force behind our words and actions needs to be love.

My dear sister, Frieda, came to celebrate my graduation with us. I remember her telling me how impressed she was with the first three speakers. Then, in good humor, how she thought that I, being the last speaker, would probably spoil it all! I was thankful when she said that she was pleasantly surprised! Graduation day, 1951, was a very happy day for me, and the presence of my sister made it all that much more special.

What made it even more special was that the institute had just recently asked me to stay on to be their full-time secretary. No worries about what I would be doing next.

As I reflect on my Bible school days, I have nothing but thankfulness for them. I learned so much, even though I still have so much more to learn. Having gotten somewhat of a grasp of what the Bible is all about was very rewarding to me. Bible school is where I decided to live for the Lord and to follow him. It gave me so much guidance on how to travel the road of life. I feel confident that my journey would have been much different and less fulfilling were it not for those special four years. It is also where my husband found me!

If any young person is reading this, I highly recommend that you consider spending at least one year at an evangelical Bible school or college. You will be thankful for all eternity that you did.

18

Happenings Back Home

Meanwhile, some major changes had happened on the farm during my Bible school days. Frieda had boarded with a family in town to take her tenth and eleventh grades. She also had worked as a telephone operator in Lintlaw for a short time. Other things were happening too! After my first year in Bible school, she contacted me and asked me if I would be her bridesmaid! I knew she and Hans had been dating, so it was no surprise.

I made my own long dress out of a heavy blue lace-like fabric. The wedding took place on July 28, 1948.

Frieda's wedding: Marian, Margaret, Alfred, Hansie, Otto, Ann, Hans, Frieda, Me, Tillie, Tom and his children

Frieda's groom was Hans, Auntie's adopted son. It was a unique and a happy arrangement for the whole family. Frieda married a man who had, in a sense, been her sibling since she was about age eleven. Interestingly, now Auntie was not only her aunt but also her mother-in-law! All of them remained in the Bader home.

Auntie was no longer able to be involved much with the farm operations, so Hans was pretty much fully in charge. For all practical purposes, he had already inherited the farm too.

A month short of their first anniversary, Frieda and Hans welcomed their first son, Daniel (Dan), into their family. The next year, they sold the farm and moved to Crystal Springs, Saskatchewan. There, they purchased a general store with housing attached. The store was the major store in that small town and handled everything. Brother Hansie, Auntie, and Uncle moved there with them. A blacksmith shop was also purchased there by my brother, Hansie, or jointly with Frieda's husband, Hans. Frieda and the kids operated the store, and the two Hanses worked in the shop. However, there wasn't enough work in the shop for both of them, so Hans took a job at a service station.

Thirteen months after Dan was born, Judy arrived. Initially she was not a healthy baby. Before long she was a healthy little tyke. Grandma Bader (Auntie) was delighted with her new role as Grandma. From the time Dannie was born, everyone called her "Granny."

Granny with Dan and Judy

74

With these two small babies and her responsibilities in the store, I was quite amazed and thrilled that Frieda had still taken time off and had come to my graduation ceremony and celebration.

My graduating class at TRBI, 1951. Second row on the far right is Principal Bruce Wannop and in the front row second from far right is me and my roommate Vivian on my right.

19

On Staff at TRBI

I had no trouble adjusting to my job as secretary. While I was taking over, Erna Klassen remained as a secretary for a while. Having worked in the office during my student years meant that I had become well-acquainted with what had to be done and was ready to do the job. That meant doing the bookkeeping, being in charge of the mail and monies received, administering the school's store, being secretary to the principal and the treasurer, helping with editing the school paper, and printing and mailing it. Added to that, I was the receptionist for anyone who came to visit the principal or the school. People had to go through my office to get to the principal's office.

The printer we used was a cylinder with grooves all around it. Metal letters and characters had to be inserted one by one into the grooves. The paper was inserted in the bottom of the machine. The cylinder was turned by hand with a handle, and the printed documents would come out. It was a very tedious and meticulous job. Later, a mimeograph machine was procured.

As the school opening came closer, Mr. Wannop asked me to teach a Christian education class to the Bible school students. The following year, he also asked me to teach a typing and a bookkeeping class. By then, I had some additional help in the office.

It is interesting that one of my students in the typing class was Cliff who later became my husband. I used to feel sorry for him because he had badly scarred and contracted muscles in his fingers on the insides of his hands. He had placed them on a hot stove when he was a toddler. Nonetheless, he still managed to learn to type somewhat and passed the class. Because typing was such a chore for him and handwriting so much easier and quicker, he soon discontinued typing, thinking he would never be able to do it at a practical level. However, now at eighty-eight years of age, the sinews in his figures have loosened up considerably, and he can now type well enough to help with such things as editing (which he is now doing on this account).

This has meant that all of these past years, he has just written everything out by hand. That included such things as his dissertation, thesis, papers, lectures, assignments for his classes, his correspondence, and eventually, his articles and books. I typed them all for him, but not until after we were married. His department's secretary would do tests and exams if she received sufficient advanced notice, which was not in the cards too often!

You might be interested in knowing that while he was taking the class from me, there were no romantic inclinations on either of our parts—at least I don't think so. But he was pretty smart, and maybe he saw something in me at that time that he did not forget!

During my time at TRBI, I received a call from home, informing me that my Uncle John was in the hospital and was dying. Never having known of him to ever have attended church, I was concerned about the destiny of his soul. I hopped on a bus and went home to see him. I tried to talk to him about Jesus and that he had died for him to pay the penalty for his sins—as well as for all of us—and that all we have to do is accept God's pardon. But he interrupted me and wouldn't hear of it. Just at the moment when I said that, a doctor entered the room, and Uncle said to him in an angry tone of voice and pointing to me, "She is trying to tell me about Jesus." The doctor never responded, and I left heartbroken for him.

That visit with my uncle has never left me. Realizing from the Bible how important it is to accept Jesus before we die, his seeming failure to do so has haunted me ever since. It causes me to want to persuade people to accept God's provision for their salvation long before the time of death arrives and while they are still able to make a thoughtful decision about the matter.

My uncle died soon after I left him. His son, Hans, later told me and some of my siblings that he had a difficult death. Hans asked the doctor to sedate him. He did, and my uncle never woke up again. I was glad that I saw him that one last time.

20

Two Big Blows

The Two Rivers Bible Institute was nestled in the forks between where the Carrot and Leather Rivers met. During the years while Cliff and I were at the school, those small rivers were unable to contain all the water flowing into them when rapid snowmelts occurred or during very heavy rainfalls. Contributing to the problem was the fact that as more land was brought under cultivation, it made the snow melt much more rapidly. Huge drainage ditches were also built that channeled water more rapidly into the rivers. Consequently, flooding occurred or seriously threatened to occur almost every year from 1948 until the institute was forced to completely abandon its site by 1956.

One of the worst of these floods occurred in 1948. The water rose up to the roofs of some of the homes on the lower elevations on campus. The barnyards, pastures, access roads, and bridges to the institute were all submerged. Except by boat, the school became completely isolated, cut off from the rest of the world. It was chaos. The main buildings, however, were on a high enough wedge of land so that the water never entered them but did come within a few feet of also doing so during the most severe floods.

While there was the threat of a flood most years from 1949 to 1953 after the 1948 flood, it was not until 1954 that the next really severe one occurred. It was a three-phase flood. Some homes had to be evacuated three times. Because of this continued threat of flooding and of the actual flooding, the majority of the institute's board reluctantly decided that it had to move the school to a new location.

Mr. Wannop, however, resisted the thought of relocating this thriving enterprise. Having poured so much of himself into the school for so many years, plus the thought of what all that dismantling and rebuilding would entail, made it unthinkable for him to agree to it.

By this time, the institute consisted of four relatively large classroom/residence hall buildings, about ten faculty residences, some married student residences, a substantial farm and pasture complex of about 200 acres, a large garden, a playfield area, an outdoor swimming pool (the swimming pool was especially important for the institute's summer youth camping program), a thriving school, etc. With limited resources, moving all of this would be such a huge undertaking. However, because of the severity of the 1954 flood, the board insisted that it had no realistic alternative but to relocate the school. Given Wannop's continued lack of readiness to agree, the board asked him to resign.

While the institute was able to continue to operate haphazardly at that site for the next two years, the slow laborious process of dismantling and relocating everything got underway. The floods were such a huge blow to the institute, and to this day, it has never fully recovered. I retained my job for the next year until I left to get married!

Wannop's departure was a big blow to me personally as well. The Wannops had become like my third second family. They even invited me to join them on their vacation trips a couple of times through Alberta and British Columbia.

One time, when dormitory living seemed to be getting to me, they invited me to stay with them for a while. During my last year at the institute, Mr. Wannop's dad, who had also moved to the institute and became part of the staff, invited me to move into the upstairs of his home. It consisted of two large rooms with a kitchenette. After living in my small dorm room for nearly six years, that was such a welcome treat. I loved it.

21

That Guy, Cliff—Who Was He Really?

In his senior year at Bible School, Cliff began coming up to the office rather frequently. Often, it seemed for rather inconsequential things. I eventually figured out why! By this time, the school had considerably relaxed their rules regarding dating for the senior Bible school students. Cliff and I were allowed to meet on Sunday afternoons in the home of one of the faculty members while they were away ministering at a church.

That guy Cliff!

That was pretty much our dating outings before Cliff graduated that spring of 1955. But it worked! Somewhere along the line, he proposed to me, and we decided to get married in August. After graduation, he went to work on a farm in Kindersley, Saskatchewan, until August. It was quite a long ways away, so I was pretty much on my own in preparing for our wedding.

During those visits, we got to know each other pretty well. We talked about our future. Cliff's original goal was to eventually work in a Bible School in some administrative capacity. In whatever capacity he eventually ended up working in, he wanted to be able to contribute to the elevation of its academic standards. That had become a felt need on the part of most Bible schools at the time. To be able to help with that, Cliff desired to further his education at a school that offered an accredited degree. What he had earned from TRBI was only a diploma. At the recommendation of a friend, he applied to Northwestern College in Minneapolis. I was willing to follow and support Cliff wherever God would lead us.

Cliff's Dad and Mom with Cliff

We talked about both of our backgrounds. It was interesting to learn that Cliff's parents were immigrants from Europe too, and that they were pioneer farmers with the same limited circumstances that I had in my childhood. He had also experienced several deaths in his family. His dad, Fritz, had been raised in Neustadt, Germany, and came to Canada in 1924. He eventually met Amalie "Molly" Schick, also an immigrant from Germany. They were married in 1931. The story is that she had told Cliff's dad that she wouldn't marry him until he had built a house for them. With the help of mainly her two brothers, Rudolf and Alfred, also recent immigrants, a nice log house was built quickly. This was in the Parkdale School District near Glaslyn, Saskatchewan.

They had four children. Cliff was born in 1932, Don in 1934, Esther in 1938, and Elizabeth (Betty) in 1942.

Cliff's Dad and Mom with Don, Cliff, and baby
Esther beside his first pick-up truck, 1939

When Betty was just nine months old, Amalie died suddenly. It was from a perforated gallbladder and the negligence of an intoxicated doctor.

When Amalie realized that she was probably going to die, she asked her unmarried sister, Freda, to take care of her children. Quite logically, it wasn't too long after that in January 1944 that Fritz and Freda were married. Sadly, that marriage lasted only about three months. Freda, too, became ill and died suddenly of a brain hemorrhage. Cliff was only eleven years old by the time he had lost not only his mom but also his aunt/stepmother.

Fritz, desperate to have some help with raising his four young children, was able to find and hire a housekeeper, Emma (Fuchs) Kitlitz. She was a widow with three children—George, Diena, and Alex. They were a little younger than Cliff and his siblings. Fritz and Emma married rather quickly after that too.

That happened after the nine of them had moved across the province and eventually settled in the Meadowcroft School District near Carrot River. Interestingly, it was just about twenty-five miles from TRBI. Incidentally, Carrot River was our first stop the night of our wedding. More on that later.

Fritz and Emma had five more children. They were Freda, David, Ruth, Fred, and Edwin. Now they had his children, her children, and their children!

Cliff's siblings: Betty, Cliff, Esther, Don, Diena,
Fred, Edwin, David, Freda, and Ruth

All of this became a little much for Emma, and some turmoil developed in the family as well. Before too long, Cliff and his brother, Don, were old enough to leave home for work and did. They were fifteen and thirteen. Fritz's two oldest girls, Esther and Betty, were sent to live elsewhere. The loving Henry Blinkin family took Esther, and Betty was equally lovingly welcomed into the home of the J. M. "Max" Baxters. The Baxters were members of the faculty at TRBI.

While living in the Meadowcroft area, all of the Maier/Kitlitz children who were old enough attended a one-room schoolhouse just like I once did. During the cold winter months, they all packed into a caboose with Cliff or his brother, Don, being the teamsters. Cliff finished his grade eight in the spring of 1947. His dad considered that to be adequate education for him. At the time, so did Cliff.

The following winter, Cliff worked with his dad in the woods, skidding pulpwood into piles and helping to load it onto big trucks to be hauled into town and loaded onto railroad cars. At the time, Cliff thought that this might be the kind of work he would be doing the rest of his life—or farming.

When that job in the woods ended that spring of 1948, his dad learned through his pastor, a TRBI graduate, that TRBI was looking for summer help. He contacted the school, and they readily accepted the offer of Cliff's help. When Cliff's dad dropped him off there, he expected that he would be picking him up to bring him back home again in the fall. Surprise! Not so. Guess why?

Starting in the summer of 1948, Cliff and I were both summer workers at TRBI. Without being particularly attracted to Cliff during those several summers, a person couldn't help but notice how diligent Cliff was at doing whatever was at hand to do, what a hard worker he was, how dependable he was, and how willingly he did any job he could, no matter how menial. Different faculty members would comment about how great a job Cliff was doing. One faculty member said, "I believe Cliff will go a long way!"

Spiritually too, his conduct was exemplary. For example, during the summer months, he chose to attend the Wednesday night prayer meetings with some of his coworkers while some of the others chose to play softball or whatever. It was obvious, however, that he also enjoyed camaraderie and participation in some hard-fought games.

He told me that he had been persuaded by that same pastor to attend a camp for young people at TRBI in 1946. He said that he had given his heart to Christ at that camp. He felt that this particular experience had a deep impact on his attitude toward many things. It was a prime reason why he felt so much at home when he was a summer worker at TRBI.

Well, surprise, surprise! As the fall approached, it became evident to Cliff that some of the guys he had been working with all summer planned to attend high school at TRBI during the upcoming school year. Cliff was kind of surprised at first. More education was not on his radar, and he had hardly been aware that TRBI had a high school. He discovered that he could exchange his work of the past summer for his expenses for the coming school year at high school. Not really realizing what he was getting himself into, Cliff decided to go too. At least it was something to do for the winter.

Little did he realize that the consequences of that decision would change the trajectory of his whole life and launch him into years of more education. His dad was baffled by it all, not only at the time but for years to come. However, as a Christian, he gradually understood that people moved by God can sometimes do things that at the moment don't make sense to the natural mind.

Cliff went on to complete his high school at TRBI. He discovered that he loved studying and became a model student and made good grades. TRBI and provincial policy obligated TRBI's grade eleven and twelve high school students to take the provincial final exams. Cliff and Jake Froese, a study partner who became a life-long friend, passed them with flying colors, as they say.

Cliff then perhaps surprisingly decided to take three years of Bible school education there as well. He told me that he decided to do so because of the good impact he saw it was having on other students. He had also come to feel the need to increase his own knowledge of the Bible and had found that he had been too busy while in high school to do much of that.

Cliff excelled in Bible School, got top grades, and became a school leader. He was elected president of his class and also became president of the Friday Night Young People's group.

All in all, I saw Cliff as a person who was diligent, a hard worker, and sincere; but most of all, also a person who truly loved the Lord and wanted to serve him. And he loved me! By the time of our marriage, I didn't want to marry anyone else, even though we were about four years separated age-wise! He was handsome, too, and had a beautiful smile which sometimes made my heart skip a beat!

22

Wedding Plans

That summer of 1955, I began preparing for our wedding. I had planned to resign before long, but Mr. Pete Schroeder, who was now in charge of the administrative aspects of the school, asked me to continue on as secretary until the week before the wedding. He promised that if I did that, the school would take care of the wedding preparations, including decorations and the meal. I agreed. I just had to concern myself about my dress and invitations. But I had no money or very little.

Again, God provided. My former roommate, Vivian, who was a size ten, and I was a size sixteen then, told me that I could have her dress and could do anything I wanted with it.

Its design made alterations manageable. I went to Prince Albert to shop for lace to match the dress; I also got some netting. Dear Dorothy Koop, a great seamstress and a faculty member, offered to do the remake. She inserted a strip of lace all the way from the sleeves down to the end of the lace on both sides. The lace only went about halfway down the skirt. The bottom was netting. She removed that old netting and replaced it with the new to make it the right length for me. And, bravo, the dress fit perfectly. Nobody would have guessed it was a remake.

Vivian and Everett Nichel   Me and Cliff
Size 10 to size 16 make over

I recently (in 2021) received an e-mail from Dorothy Koop's daughter, now Brown, and in it she reminisced about her mom's experience of remaking my dress. She wrote:

> I well remember the wedding gown my mom prayed over as she made it fit the precious bride she had come to love. How she was able to fit that project into her busy schedule and get it done in the packed full little cabin where we lived is beyond me. But she was up to the challenge. Bless her heart!

For the corsage, I wanted to carry a white Bible with a floral arrangement on top of it. Another friend offered to make the corsage. My sister, Frieda, loaned me the veil she wore. I was set!

What about a going-away outfit? God provided that too. Dave Neufeld, who had worked with me in the office for a while, gave me

$50 for the express purpose of purchasing a going-away outfit. He later became a Rena Ware Cookware salesman, and he and his wife also presented us with a beautiful heavy-duty stainless-steel set of cookware as our wedding gift. I am still using parts of that cookware today—sixty-five years later!

One more thing—our wedding cake. In our tradition, we used fruit cakes for the wedding cake. I asked my aunt and Frieda if they would provide the cake. Granny declined, but Frieda said, "We can do that for her." And she did. We picked up three round cakes, all different sizes, and took them to the Tisdale Bakery to be decorated. It was a beautiful three-tier cake. The owner of the bakery was a supporter of TRBI and said, "No charge!"

You might wonder why I was so broke? What did I do with my salary? Well, there was no salary. As with all the staff, we all worked as volunteers "as unto the Lord." We used to say, "Our pay is out of this world" because we believed God would reward us for our voluntary labor of love.

As singles, we did receive an allowance of $3 per month in the institute's store to be used for our personal needs. During my last couple of years that I was at the school, a great couple, Ed and Fern Jackson, who attended one of the churches where the school ministered on Sundays, began sending me $10 every once in a while. It helped me a lot.

I was so blessed when I would read verses like Matthew 10:42 where it says that even giving a cup of cold water to a child will be rewarded. Jesus's own words in Matthew 25 starting at verse 31 are so amazing. He states that little things like feeding the hungry, giving a drink, inviting in a stranger, giving someone clothing, visiting and caring for the sick, and even visiting someone in prison are noticed by Jesus, pleases him, and will be rewarded. This along with his command to love him with our whole heart, mind, soul, and strength and my appreciation for his great gift of salvation made working without pay a joy.

23

Our Wedding and Honeymoon

The wedding date of August 10 was not far away. I asked my niece, Gladys, to be my bridesmaid, and Cliff asked his best friend, George Baxter, to be his best man. I asked Frieda if two of her children, Danny and Judy, would be ring bearer and flower girl respectively. She agreed, and that pleased Granny. Mr. Art Linsey, a TRBI faculty member, agreed to officiate the wedding.

The night before our wedding, the sky was almost "black." Everyone feared the worst. If it rained, the dirt roads into the school would be virtually impassable. Knowing the character of the mud in that area, almost no one would venture into it. I got down on my knees and "put out a fleece" to the Lord. I asked him to give us the most beautiful day tomorrow and so confirm that our marriage was indeed his will for us.

The day came, and the weather was absolutely perfect.

Guests came—about two hundred of them! They included my aunt (Granny), Frieda and Hans and their family, my brother, Tom, and his family, sister Ann and her husband, Rudy, and brothers Alfred and Otto. Only brother Hansie couldn't make it. And amazingly, the Quarks came all the way from Ontario to be at our wedding. If we would have known that they were coming, we would certainly have had him officiate at the wedding.

Our wedding
George, Cliff, Me, Gladys, and Dan and Judy Bader

The tabernacle, the institute's auditorium, was attractively decorated with wild ferns, flowers, and candles. Beautiful! The dining room was decorated as beautifully as I had ever seen it. The meal was delicious! Mr. Schroeder had certainly kept his promise of doing these preparations if I stayed on longer at the school as their secretary.

Mr. Schroeder had planned a short program for after dinner. A boat had been decorated with crepe paper, and we were asked to sit in it, symbolizing our launch into our new life together. All the flooding that had been occurring may have prompted the idea of a boat! He said afterward, "It couldn't have been a more beautiful day."

We were lavished with gifts. Mr. Schroeder's wife, Ann, said that she had never seen a couple so well outfitted. Even though there was no wedding registry, we received no duplicates. Quite amazing. In addition to the gifts, we received $400 in cash from various friends. Grandpa Wannop gave us $50, a big gift for those days. My aunt gave us an electric tea kettle, and Frieda, in addition to the wedding cake, gave us an electric iron. These are two items that we have used a lot and which have been replaced several times over the years.

George Baxter loaned us his car to go on our honeymoon. That honeymoon started with going to Cliff's dad's home just north of Carrot River for the evening. For some reason, he couldn't make the wedding and asked us to come in our wedding attire. We set out, and some distance from a stop sign, I said, "Stop!" Cliff thought that I was already doing "some backseat driving," so he just continued on until we did reach the stop sign.

When he stopped, I quickly pushed open the door and vomited violently. He felt so bad. He tried to comfort me. After things subsided considerably, we proceeded on to his dad's place. When we got there, I continued doing some vomiting, this time over the banister outside of his dad's house. Finally, Cliff went for some medicine from the drugstore. Things then settled down somewhat.

That was the way our first night together began. We spent the rest of the night in the only hotel in that small town of Carrot River—not exactly a five-star one. With me not knowing when I would be sick again, our first night was not the greatest.

The day after our wedding, we drove to Prince Albert to stay with my sister, Ann, and her husband for a few days. I know. They had to be gone to work all day. We had the place to ourselves most of the time. But how could that be much of a fun honeymoon? Perhaps, surprisingly, for me, it was. Having been more or less isolated at the institute for eight years, being in a "big" city and in a modern home was indeed special for me. All in all, our Prince Albert stop proved to be a great start to our honeymoon!

When we returned to TRBI to pack for Minneapolis, to our horror, we discovered that it was not only I who was sick after our wedding day dinner, but many others were too. In fact, Granny, my brother, Tom, and Grandpa Wannop were so sick that they were afraid they would die. We were devastated. Apparently, the pressed chicken that the ladies had prepared for the dinner had spoiled. They had prepared it a couple of days earlier and placed it into a cooler, but the refrigeration was inadequate. For years after that, whenever we returned home, invariably, someone would remind us of that dinner at our wedding.

We got out my old wooden suitcase along with a couple of other suitcases and packed our treasures. The only things of this world's goods that we owned apart from these newly acquired gifts were our clothes and books from our Bible School days.

We said our goodbyes to our family at TRBI. It was a sad and happy occasion. It seemed like the school was on the verge of experiencing some

Three main buildings of TRBI when we left

great turmoil and even chaos with all the uncertainties surrounding the proposed imminent relocation. Would school be cancelled to facilitate the move? Would the school survive? Would a faculty and staff remain available? Who would take on the office responsibilities? So many uncertainties!

On the other hand, though torn, Cliff and I were excited to be taking off, boarding the train, finishing our honeymoon, and heading for Minneapolis. The trip was special. On the way, we stopped in Winnipeg. While there, we purchased a typewriter! Since Granny had treated me to that first typewriter, life had become impossible without one for me! On the train, we treated ourselves to dining in the luxury diner. We were excited, thrilled, and full of anticipation to begin our new life together in a totally different and new environment.

24

Northwestern College, Minneapolis

When we arrived in Minneapolis, we were greeted by four friends who had once also been students at TRBI. One was Cliff's good friend, George, who had been his best man at our wedding, along with his wife, Ethel. The other two were Ray and Tena Dell. Both of the guys were also furthering their education and were enrolled at Northwestern College. Northwestern was a Christian nondenominational liberal arts college.

The Dells had reserved an apartment for us right across the hall from theirs. It didn't take long for us to unpack and settle in. Both of these couples had a car. The Dells would take us shopping for groceries when they went.

Right across the street from our apartment was Loring Park, beautiful at that time. Northwestern College also fronted on Loring Park, and so did the former headquarters of the Billy Graham Evangelistic Association. Factors such as these helped to make us feel at home. We were happy as larks—we could hardly have been happier and truly loving our newfound life and lifestyle.

Cliff immediately enrolled for classes and decided that history would be his major. Northwestern had some great instructors. Cliff was fortunate to discover some of them early—people like John Dahlin, William Growler, J. Edwin Hartill, William Bernsten, Mark W. Lee, and Edwin Olson.

He quickly obtained a job as well. It was parking cars for a large department store in downtown Minneapolis. He worked at that for almost two years. Following the winter semester of 1957, he obtained a full-time job with Northwest Airlines as a baggage handler, food loader/unloader. and plane guide. I also quickly obtained a job as a bookkeeper at the Butler's Drug Store.

Cliff enjoyed his classes at Northwestern, but along with everything else there was to become logically involved in, he was very busy. He found that some of the classes were very demanding. For example, while Professor Dahlin was an excellent and interesting teacher, his assignments approached the level of graduate courses. For a survey course, he assigned extensive reading, research, and a documented term paper. While Cliff enjoyed this type of studying, it just was very time-consuming.

I had more time on my hands but kept busy with the household routine and work. However, Cliff began using a vocabulary that was foreign to me. I began to feel left behind, so before the first semester was over, I asked myself the question, "Why don't I also go to school?" Cliff was in agreement. But a problem: I didn't have my high school diploma. Fortunately, the school had a policy that a person over twenty-five could enroll if they passed an entrance exam. I took the exam. Believe me, it was a struggle, but I passed. So, the next semester, I enrolled and chose Christian education as my major.

We enjoyed life in Minneapolis. It was the first big city we had lived in. There was so much to see—the relatively large number of lakes in the area, the mighty Mississippi flowing through it, the skyscrapers and the huge department stores with their glistening enviable wares, the beautiful parks—so different and too much to list!

We frequently got together with the two couples we knew from TRBI. The guys were both fun-loving kind of guys. We also began a Canadian Club and met more Canadians. Of course, we also met great Americans. One was Diane (Sutton) Case who graciously consented to play the piano for our club get-togethers. Unbelievably, she, like us, later in life, turned up here in Marquette and presently (2021) is the organist at our church. She has become one of our dear friends. While in Minneapolis, we also attended church regularly and established some great friendships there too.

To our astonishment, during our second year at Northwestern, the school began experiencing some serious conflict over whether or not to become an accredited institution. We had gone to Northwestern with the understanding that negotiations to that end were well underway and would succeed during the first year we were there. Some board members, including the school's president and some of its faculty, wanted that to be the case. Some did not. It turned out that the view of the latter group was strong enough to cause the effort to collapse. The president and some of the faculty resigned over it.

We were perplexed. One of Cliff's desires and great concerns had been to obtain a degree from an accredited school. One of our professors, Mark W. Lee, was one of the faculty members who resigned and obtained a position at an accredited institution, Whitworth College (now University), in Spokane, Washington. He also became the pastor at the Evangelical Free Church there. Having become aware of our situation, he invited Cliff and me to consider Whitworth too. We applied and were accepted conditionally. Whitworth agreed to accept the credits that we had earned at Northwestern if we maintained a B or above average during our first year.

By the end of our second year at Northwestern, we had somehow saved enough money to purchase our first old but nice-looking car. We were quite proud of it. Before we left for Washington State, we received a call early one morning. The party on the other end informed us that he had run into the back of our parked car the night before and gave us the information we needed to collect our insurance. Fortunately for us, the car was not damaged so badly that it could not continue to be used without fixing it. We used the money for other things.

Interestingly, later in Seattle, another one of our cars was also hit in the rear. The damage on it too was not so severe that it could not continue to be used without fixing it. We again collected the insurance but didn't repair the car. We have often joked that it was one of the ways that we financed our "higher education!"

Before we left Minneapolis, Cliff was able to arrange to have his full-time job with Northwest Airlines transferred to Spokane.

25

Whitworth College, Spokane

Time came to load up a U-Haul trailer and leave Minneapolis for Spokane. What an interesting trip it was, traveling across parts of America we had never seen before nor had even imagined existed. It was a 1,380-mile trip across the vast expanse of parklands and plains of Northern Minnesota and North Dakota, the rugged Bad Lands of Eastern Montana, and then through the majestic mountains of Western Montana and Idaho. We finally reached beautiful Lake Coeur d'Alene in Western Idaho and then Whitworth College in the pine groves of Eastern Washington. What a beautiful campus it was. Our little old "remodeled" car had gotten us there without a single breakdown. We thanked God.

Whitworth was of the more conservative variety of Presbyterians that existed in America at that time. That was generally true of Presbyterian churches on the west coast. They often had outstanding spiritual pastors such as Robert B. Munger, author of the book *My Heart: Christ's Home*. Frank F. Warren, president of Whitworth at the time, was an extraordinary conservative and spiritual individual. He fostered a strong spiritual atmosphere on campus.

We checked on housing and were informed that a divorced man, who had a teenage daughter, was looking for a couple to live at his place free of charge and help raise his daughter and cook the evening meal. They would only be required to share in the cost of the groceries. It sounded like a good way to make it possible for both of us to continue our education, so we accepted the offer.

We both enrolled in college, and Cliff resumed his full-time job with Northwest Airlines. Living at that home, however, was an unpleasant experience. The family was messy and had a dog that they didn't care for properly. In January, I got pregnant and found it difficult to tolerate the loud music the daughter would play into all hours of the night. Finally, that spring, we rented an apartment in the married student housing complex on Whitworth's campus. That was a very pleasant change.

As September 1958 came, it was not only time to enroll in school again, but it was also getting close to my due date. Rather reluctantly, however, I enrolled for school. About two weeks after school started, our precious baby arrived.

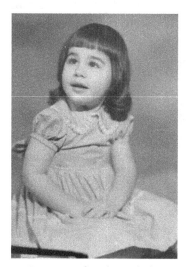

Fern, our first born baby

I can't express the feelings I felt when I first saw her. Only mothers can know it. She had such a beautiful face and long black hair. The nurses put a red ribbon in it. We named her Fern Carol after Fern Jackson who helped support me while I was at Two Rivers, and Carol just because we liked the name. I was in a room with two other mothers. One nurse, when she first saw Fern, said that she just had to find out who the mother of that beautiful baby was. I think she was shocked when she discovered that it was me!

Cliff couldn't experience those first few moments with me because when I had my children, the fathers still had to sit out in a waiting room until the doctor came out and made the announcement, "You are now the proud father of a daughter or a son."

I returned to class a week after Fern was born. The professor was surprised to see me so soon. He had me stand and congratulated me, and the class applauded. I had no problem finding someone to care for her the hour or so I was in class. Our neighbors were just like family, and everyone loved our baby!

Our stay in that married student apartment at Whitworth was an especially happy time for us. I had the joy and pleasure of taking care of my baby without going to a job. We socialized with other couples and have kept in touch with a couple of them for years. Cliff was especially busy, though. It is amazing how he could work full-time, carry a full load of studies, and still keep up with his assignments and make good grades.

It was a great day when graduation day came in May 1959. We both walked in the procession, and both of us graduated cum laude.

Both of us graduate with BA degrees and baby Fern

What made it even more special was the surprise appearance of a couple of good friends from Saskatchewan, Pete and Ann Schroeder, from our good old TRBI days. He was the one who arranged the

Ann, Billie, and Pete Schroeder

preparations for our wedding. They had come all the way from Saskatchewan. We were rather dumbfounded and at the same time very thrilled.

What would be next? Some of Cliff's professors strongly recommended that he go on to get his master's degree. After much thought, he decided that he should. From Spokane, the University of Washington in Seattle was the most logical place to apply. He did and was accepted.

During the last year while we were living in Spokane, we decided to take advantage of a great perk that Northwestern Airlines offered their employees. We could get a free pass on its airline to anywhere in the United States. We decided to go to New York and Miami. The Milton Erways, who had been professors at Northwestern then at Whitworth during our first year there and had moved to New York, had invited us to visit them there (we babysat and housesat for them in Spokane while they were on vacation). We accepted Erway's offer. Initially, we had planned to take Fern with us. But a great couple at the Evangelical Free Church, which we attended, offered to take care of her while we were gone.

When we got to New York, the Erways spent the best part of a week taking us to many of the tourist attractions in the city. We then flew to Miami and loved the views and the beautiful weather. We thoroughly enjoyed that trip.

26

The University of Washington and Early Seattle Days

To get to Seattle, we again utilized a small U-Haul trailer. When we arrived, we found an apartment that I swear had the world's smallest kitchen. It was cubical in shape. The sink, stove, and fridge touched at their corners, and there was room only for one person to stand in it. We stayed there for only a very short time while we looked for an apartment complex that we could manage in exchange

Fern learns to ride a
tricycle with Dad

for free rent. We found one with eleven units. For managing the complex, they gave us free rent, including all utilities. Our apartment had three large rooms and was partially furnished. We shared a bathroom with one person. It also had a nice backyard.

Cliff almost immediately found a job with a concrete pipe construction company in Renton, Washington. It was quite a drive from where we lived but doable, and the pay was good. Northwest Airlines was too far away to continue working with that company.

One of our first priorities, too, was to find a good church. We were contacted by a very warm evangelical Presbyterian couple who informed us that the University Presbyterian Church was a good solid Bible-believing church. We found it to be very welcoming. Almost immediately, we made it our church home and quickly made some lasting friendships. One special blessing was that at that church, we found a retired nurse who was happy to babysit for us. While I hated to go to work and leave my baby to be cared for by someone else, we felt good about that babysitter.

I quickly found a job at the North Pacific Coast Freight Bureau as secretary to the manager. I can remember when I was interviewed, the assistant manager dictated a short letter to me to transcribe. In it, he used the name of the company a couple of times. I think he was surprised that I could keep up with him so well and keep things straight. The key was that I just wrote N and P in shorthand for the whole name. The symbol in shorthand for N is just a dash and for P an elongated bracket. So I just wrote N and crossed it with P in shorthand for the whole name. I think he was impressed. At any rate, he hired me on the spot. I enjoyed my job. It was a very pleasant work environment, and the pay and benefits were very good.

27

Day Care

Cliff enrolled at the University of Washington and settled into his routine of studies and work. Then about a month later, I got pregnant with my second child. I never suffered with morning sicknesses during my pregnancies so had no problem working. I was intending to quit about three weeks before the due date, but my boss asked me to stay on until the week before it. The job would be waiting for me when I returned. To our amazement, we were informed that the company had a perk that paid mothers employed by the company $1,000 for each birth. For us, that was a lot of money.

When our baby was ready to come, it was quite sudden and unexpected. Cliff was away at work. I felt quite an urgency, so I called a cab. He nervously told me that he couldn't help me if I needed any before we got to the hospital. When we arrived, he just rushed me in. He didn't want me to take time to pay him. I don't think I ever did! He was just glad to get me off of his hands! When I got to the delivery area, the nurses seemed to be just as nervous. They rushed me into the delivery room without prepping me. I could feel the baby coming, but I couldn't see the doctor. I said, "Where is the doctor? It's coming!"

While putting his mask on, he went from the head of my bed to the foot. Before he finished tying on his mask, our beautiful first son had arrived. I have often said that Virgil was in a hurry when he came, and he has been ever since. We named him George Virgil— George after Cliff's best friend, and Virgil after the doctor who "almost" delivered him.

Our first born son, Virgil

As I thought of motherhood, I never envisioned letting some-one else raise my children. Now I had two—what would I do? I

Me with daughter Fern loving on baby brother Virgil

decided to begin a day care center. In that way, I could raise my own children and still add a bit to the family income. I just charged twenty-five cents an hour! I attended a seminar on starting a day care center. Two things I learned that were especially useful was doing finger-painting and making my own Play-Doh.

I put an ad in the paper. I soon had four children to take care of. Three were from couples, and one was from a single parent, Olive. She and I would become lifelong best friends.

We went to St. Vincent's and equipped our living room for play school. We found a long low table, children's kitchen equipment, and all sorts of toys. I wanted things that would teach children to be creative like tinker toys, erector sets, Lincoln Logs, building blocks, puzzles, etc. We purchased children's records to play music and had an ample supply of children's books.

In our routine, we usually spent some time outdoors, playing games, or just let them have fun.

I would usually have a finger-painting time and Play-Doh time. The kids were occupied all the time. We always had a quiet time for about an hour in the afternoon. That would not only give the kids but also me some extra energy. The kids had a good time. In fact, sometimes two of them would cry when a parent came to pick them up to go home.

Day care children minus two in front of my dryer!

Our church was important to us. We joined a Friday Night Bible Study consisting of four couples. It was also a great diversion from caring for the children all week. We would take turns meeting in each other's homes. The other couples were all well-employed and had beautiful homes. One was an engineer at Boeing, and his wife was a nurse; another was an architect, and his wife was also a nurse; the other two were older, and both were teachers. Only the older couple had children, and they were gone. We hesitated to take our turn in having the study at our apartment, but we did. One couple, Tom and Jean Crosley, especially Jean, really befriended me. She gave me her going-away clothes that she had grown out of. When she replaced a small appliance, she would give me the old one. She came to visit me on occasion. I can remember her asking me if I had a problem with being in my circumstances when all the rest of the group were so well-established. That did get me feeling a little depressed at times.

One of the couples, Don and Claudia Diebert, took us on as a mission project and gave us $10 every month all the time that Cliff was in school. One time, they had the church give us a Thanksgiving basket with a turkey and all the trimmings for a great Thanksgiving meal. My feelings were mingled as I received it—glad yet sort of embarrassed that we were on the list of the needy.

28

Baby Number Three

Soon, I would add one more to our number of children. I became pregnant again. One of my keenly felt needs was to learn how to drive. I had failed two attempts previously. During my eighth month of this pregnancy, Cliff took me to the driver's training site to give it another try. On the way, I thought if I don't make it this time, I will give up. The instructor told me to get into the car. I had a hard time fitting in under the steering wheel. He asked me to parallel park. Oops, I knocked over the posts! I thought that was it, but he told me to proceed. When we returned, he told me I could go in and get my license.

Surprised, I said, "I passed?"

"Yes, but you need to practice parallel parking!" I think he felt sorry for me being as pregnant as I was at the time.

When delivery time was approaching, I began feeling the need to go to the hospital. Again, Cliff was a long ways away at work. I felt that I could hold it off until the mothers came to pick up their children. I then asked Olive if she would take care of Fern and Virgil until Cliff came home. She couldn't get me off to the hospital fast enough. Again, I went by cab, but this time, it didn't seem so urgent. The cab driver was calm! And I did pay him! It was several hours before Mark arrived.

Happy third child, Mark

We named him Mark Warren—Mark after our professor friend, Mark Lee, at both Northwestern and Whitworth. We have stayed in touch with him all of these years since then. The baby's second name, Warren, was after the great president Whitworth had while we were there.

With our adorable new baby, we felt more crowded in our apartment. The apartment next to ours was a one-room apartment that was about twenty-five feet long! We asked the owner if he would consider letting us divide it into two and make the half next to our apartment part of ours by creating an entrance from ours into it. He agreed. Guess who did the work? Our Bible Study group.

Tom, being the architect, headed it up, and in one day, we had an added bedroom. Cliff and I took the new room, and the kids had the other larger bedroom. It was a wonderful improvement.

We enjoyed our time in Seattle. On many Saturdays, we would do things like go to the zoo, the arboretum, the aquarium, or just go down to the ocean or to a lake. The kids especially loved going to the zoo.

At the zoo with Mark and me

Each time, we would see a different area of it and there were rides they could go on. We would go to some of the circuses; and when the World's Fair was on, we frequented aspects of that. We watched the Space Needle being built and took a ride to the top. Cliff was part of a nice group at school too, and they would do fun family things from time to time. Some of them had cabins and/or boats, and occasionally, we would be invited to join them.

About this time, I received a letter from my friend, Vivian Strickert, now Bruck. She was one of the two girls who came to do Vacation Bible School in the little church close to our farm when I was just a teenager. However, unexpectedly, she introduced me to a business opportunity, Amway. Knowing her standards and principles, I thought if she thought it was good, I would join. However, I just signed up one associate, my friend, Olive, and got acquainted with the products. That is about all I did with it in Seattle.

When Mark was about six months old, I received a call from Frieda in Saskatchewan, saying that my aunt Marie (Granny) was not doing well and that it was probably terminal. I chose to see her one more time while she was still alive rather than wait and just go to the funeral. Cliff was busy at school and work and was not free to take off. I reserved a berth on the train, got a bassinet for Mark, and took off with the three children. It was an overnight trip. Fern and Virgil slept in the top bunk. I put Mark in his bassinet across the bottom of my berth across my feet. Quite a challenge it all was, but I was glad I did it and was able to see her one more time and to have her meet our children too. Happily, she recuperated and lived for about another eight years. Tough "cookie" she was.

29

The Drano Catastrophe

I kept on with my usual routine of managing the apartment and taking care of the children as Cliff did with his. One time, we rented to an older man. We eventually learned, poor guy, that he was a kleptomaniac. He picked up "everything" as he walked the streets and brought it home to his apartment. His apartment was in chaos. When we realized what was happening, we first tried to get him to stop it and get rid of the stuff, but he wouldn't. Then we tried to evict him, but he wouldn't leave. So we called the police, and they took him.

The policeman said that we had to keep his things for a while, even though it all looked like garbage. We stored it in an enclosure under the back porch of our complex. It did have a door on it, but being "garbage," who would ever bother it? So why bother locking it?

The next spring, it was time for Cliff to complete his master's program by writing an exam that extended over two days. Just before that, Cliff asked me to help him with a project that would take the whole day. I hired two babysitters to take care of all the children. In the latter part of that afternoon, I called home to see how things were going. To my shock, a policeman answered the phone and said, "Call the campus police and get to the County Hospital as fast as you can. Your children have swallowed an unknown quantity of Drano."

My heart sank. When I got there, little nine-month-old Mark was crying and isolated in an oxygen tent, and Virgil was crying in a bed. What had happened was that the children were playing house in the backyard. Apparently, looking for things to feed them, they pulled open that door, got into that old man's garbage, and found a can of Drano. They thought it was rice. The older one, Debbie, tried to feed the younger ones. Fern, age four, could spit it out. Virgil, age two, got most of it out, but baby Mark just cried with it sitting on his tongue.

I was beside myself. So helpless. I could comfort Virgil but couldn't even pick up Mark. All I could do was look at my poor terrified baby boy as he pathetically looked back at me. The hospital personnel were totally inflexible. They wouldn't even consider letting me stay there at the hospital to be with my baby. They said it would be better for Mark if I wasn't there. Happily, Virgil was allowed to go home with me. Fortunately, the Drano didn't get into their voice boxes. Mark still has a scar on his tongue to this day (2021) from it.

Mark had to stay in the hospital for several days. During that time, I was allowed to visit him only briefly and then was asked to leave. The staff really didn't want me to visit him at all. They said he would be worse after I left. Eventually, however, they called me to come and feed him because he wouldn't eat from them. When we were finally able to bring him home, what a joyous day! When he was in his bed in the hospital, he looked so emaciated and looked like a starving child in a Third World country.

Immediately, when I took him into my arms, his appearance began to improve. By the time we got him out of the door of the hospital, his appearance had already improved so much, almost like nothing had happened to him. We could hardly believe our eyes. Were we ever delighted and relieved!

30

Bombshell

One night in that new bedroom, Cliff was holding me in his arms and said, "Honey, I have something to tell you. I can no longer believe what I used to believe. I have lost my faith. With regard to what we believe, I am afraid that we will never have anything in common anymore. I think maybe you should go your way and I mine." I thought this meant that because he saw things differently on matters of faith, he wanted to get out of the marriage.

I ripped myself out of his arms and said, "That's a fine how do you do! After I helped put you through school!" That is the way that conversation ended that night.

Me and Cliff, Mark, Virgil, and Fern
Our family about that time

I wondered what was next for me and the kids. Would he just not come home someday? Would he ask me to leave? Where would I go? How would I support our three kids? What would I do? Would I return to Canada?

I prayed and I cried. I was reminded of the prayer I prayed the night before our wedding when I asked God to give us a great day and thus show us that we were indeed doing his will. I concluded that separation was definitely not God's plan. It was till death do us part. My commitment to stay with the marriage was firm.

I had always thought that separation was something he never considered and his promise of "till death do us part" was as firm as mine, that he would even consider separation was a complete surprise and shock to me.

As I remember it, I was unaware of his faith crisis. Cliff is quite certain that he did share it with me prior to that night. He remembers me arguing with him about it. I do, too, but I feel it was after that night.

As Cliff remembers it, in 1962, his faith problem had been developing over about six months. He recalls how tremendously upset he was. He could see that this would end his lifelong objective of going into some kind of Christian work. Furthermore, that it could end our marriage or at the very least be very disappointing and unfair to me.

Cliff tells me that he sought help from two Christian pastors to help stop this slide into unbelief and agnosticism. His doubts, however, became stronger and more entrenched, one might say. He felt he would never again become a believer in a personal knowable God.

Cliff thinks that the reason he brought up the possibility of separating that night was because he was sure in his own mind that he had become a different person. That meant that if I was going to continue to live with him and pour my life into his, in fairness to me, I should know that. Not to level with me about his feelings would have been very hypocritical and unfair to me. He felt I should know, terrible as it would be, to learn the truth. If I no longer wanted to live with him because of that, he should give me the option to separate. The fact that he never brought up the subject of separation again told me that he was not pushing for a divorce. I never mentioned it again either.

On the religious level, however, our relationship changed. We both went about doing our activities as though that conversation about separation had never happened. In every other way, we pretty much continued to pull together as a team, although sometimes in widely separated circumstances and doing quite different things. Praise God, eventually, we would again be reunited on the religious level, but it would be fifteen years before it happened. I will relate more when we get to that period.

Cliff's conduct toward me in the years following that conversation that night proved that he loved me and admired me as much as ever for the kind of woman he tells me he thinks I am. As I look back, one of the things I am truly grateful to God for is that he gave me that kind of a husband.

How did Cliff's faith collapse? Some of you may be interested in what he has told me as to how he believes it happened. His doubts began with questions like whether or not God really answers prayer? He believes that his decline in faith began because, thinking he was too busy, he discontinued reading the Bible and praying. In doing that, he was gradually cutting himself off from God and the answers that are found in the Bible for life's situations. Simultaneously, as this was happening, he was not only ignoring the answers he once knew from the Bible but also forgetting them.

Cliff says that he became pretty much a pure rationalist, seeking to understand everything only with his mind. This was strengthened by being in an atmosphere and culture in which answers and personal help are believed to come only from reason and from human effort. In this mode of thought, a person starts to look only to one's own thoughts and efforts and no longer even thinks of the necessity of consulting God or the Bible. It is an atmosphere in which man becomes "the measure of all things" as Leonardo da Vinci is purported to have declared and is mistakenly heralded in many modern contexts.

Once this happens, a person begins to think, too, that he or she is free to determine their own morality without considering God's standards.

Cliff did still believe in God and that the fantastic design in the physical universe and that things in nature could not have happened except as the result of the work of an awesome genius Creator/Designer we call God. At the same time, he became an agnostic about certain things and, therefore, became incapable of believing the things that had once been such a certainty.

Looking back on it, he believes he had just become so busy that he continued to neglect prayer and personal Bible reading through which God has ordained that he primarily speaks to us. Consequently, his struggles concerning his faith continued.

31

More Graduate School and a Near-Death Episode

Cliff received his master's degree in 1962. It was a joyous day.

Cliff graduates with his MA degree and our three children

But, on the other hand, would he now go on to obtain a doctorate? His main graduate school adviser and director, Professor Donald

Emerson, especially was interested in seeing him do that. Cliff knew that his original goal of working in a Bible school was no longer a possibility. He had just completed six years of education since our marriage, and now, to launch into three more years with three little children seemed overwhelming to me, especially with the state of his faith. However, he decided that was what he should do. So I sort of supported his decision.

One of the reasons it took Cliff so long to get through his graduate program is that he reduced his credit hours many quarters to be able to work enough to take care of expenses. It is quite amazing that at this time, all of our educational expenses and other things were completely paid. We were totally debt-free. We didn't even have a credit card. In fact, we had never used one. If we didn't have the cash, we wouldn't buy. So we thought that we had wonderful credit! More on this later!

This lengthened time needed to finish his degree made his graduate record look bad in a sense. For this reason, and some others, Cliff never qualified for significant grants.

Another thing that extended Cliff's time in graduate school was the difficulty he had with learning foreign languages. He needed one for his master's degree and one for the doctorate. He selected French and German. He found French particularly difficult. He often also said that he had discovered that his long-term memory was really quite deficient and that he had to constantly compensate for that by doing more reviewing than was generally required of people in higher education. I didn't see any evidence of that, but then again, I was not privy to everything. The in-depth day-long "field" exams graduate students had to pass required the recall of a lot of material that a student had been required to read. Having extended his program over a longer period of time also meant that more things needed good recall. Because Cliff was afraid of not being able to recall a lot of things, he took a lot of notes. That, too, extended the time he needed to feel ready for those field exams.

In the spring of 1964, I again became pregnant. About the fourth month into the pregnancy, I began having difficulty. While I was doing the dishes one evening, I began to bleed. I then laid down on the floor and lost more blood. Fortunately, the children were already in bed. Cliff called the doctor who said it sounded like a heavy period, implying that it was not that unusual. Cliff got me settled into bed and then went upstairs to clean a vacated apartment. In about two hours, he returned and checked on me. He said, "Honey, you are green." He called the doctor again and ordered an ambulance.

I had to go to the bathroom. Cliff brought me a five-gallon bucket so I wouldn't have to walk to the bathroom. I filled it about two-thirds full of what looked like blood. It was very frightening.

When I got to the hospital, the doctor was waiting for me at the front door and began to work on me in the elevator. He did a D and C without any anesthesia, and I didn't feel anything. He said, "Young lady, you just got here in time." I was close to death.

He immediately ordered blood transfusions. I resisted, but he said, "If you don't get blood, you will be in here for six months." He gave me three of them.

The doctor kept me in the hospital for quite a while. He wouldn't let me go home and look after the children. My good friend, Jean Crosley, graciously offered to help. She said, "I can't take the children, but I can take you." I stayed at her home for three weeks. Our dear friend, Olive, helped Cliff figure out how to manage the care of the children while I was away.

I finally returned home, and life continued as usual. My miscarriage had occurred in August. Cliff continued on in his doctrinal program. Then I began experiencing some depression. The doctor sent me to a psychiatrist. By the next spring, we decided that it was time to take out a student loan to ease up on our financial burdens.

Fortunately, somehow, we learned that the government had a program in which a first-time home owner could purchase a house with no down payment. We looked into it and soon had purchased our first house. What a happy day for us! It was a one-story three-bedroom house with a fenced backyard in a pleasant neighborhood and only a few blocks from a nice little lake.

32

A Happy Development and a Shocker

We quickly settled into our new home. I now only had Olive's two children, Jennie and John, besides our own to take care of. She had a new baby. Our move meant that we were too far away from the other children to continue to take care of them. It was a treat, however, to have just five children. Olive lived on the shore on the other side of the lake. We would go over there and swim, have picnics, and just socialize with each other. Two of our close neighbors had children the same ages as ours. They soon all became friends and played with each other.

It was here that our three children started school. Because Cliff was away at school and working so much with our car and I could now drive, we purchased a second car. This meant that I could finally get my own groceries and do some things with the kids by myself.

Then in 1966, another bombshell struck. My sister, Frieda, called me, and the first thing she said was, "Hans died!" I couldn't believe it. He was only forty-eight years old, had not been sick, and they had five young children ranging in age from four to fifteen. Here my sister was, suffering almost the same devastation that my mother had. She, too, was left with five small children. I just had to go and be with her!

My brother, Otto, was living in British Columbia. I contacted him about going back to the funeral with him. Fern and Virgil were in school at the time, so I took Mark and left. I took the bus to Vancouver where Otto met me, and we drove to Saskatchewan together.

The whole situation associated with Hans' death was so sad. One day, he was sitting on the sofa and felt like he had something in his chest. He asked Frieda to boil some water to provide some steam to maybe help. She went to put the kettle on and went back into the living room. He had his head down. She lifted it up, and he breathed his last breath.

The sudden death of Hans was doubly difficult for the children. Their grandmother (Auntie Marie) had died just ten months before her son did. That was a very, very sad time for all of them. She had also been such a huge part in their lives as she was in all five of us kids (my siblings and I) when we, too, lost not only our dad but also our mom. Granny, at seventy-eight years of age, died on her knees, waxing the bathroom floor. Her granddaughter, Marilyn, who was only ten years old at the time, was the first one to find her there. She says it still haunts her. I can relate to her.

The loss and anxiety Frieda had to have suffered is hard to imagine. By this time, Hans and Frieda had moved from Crystal Springs to Prince Albert and had three more children aged ten, seven, and four. They were Marilyn, born in January 1956; Fred, born in January 1959; and Patricia, born in July 1962. Hans had left a small insurance policy, but that wouldn't carry her very far.

I stayed with Frieda for three weeks to help in any way that I could. It was amazing, though, how she rallied to the challenge that was ahead of her. Earlier, she had taken a typing class at night school in Prince Albert and had an office job. She had a great church family that supported her and some other close friends who stood by her. Unfortunately, all her siblings lived so far away that we were of little help to her. I will relate more of her story a little later.

Judy reminded me that shortly after Hans' death, we had a wonderful time with Frieda and four of her children—Judy, Marilyn, Fred, and Pattie—when they visited us in Seattle. My other sister, Ann, and her hubby, Rudy, took Frieda and the four children on a road trip with their travel trailer to see us. It was the first time any of the kids had been out of Saskatchewan. They were awed by all the sights on the way, especially the majestic mountains.

I can remember when we were showing them around the city that Judy requested to visit the SeaTac airport. None of them had ever been to an airport, let alone been on an airplane. She remembers me asking an attendant if we could peak into a jetliner. It was so exciting for them to see something like this for the first time. Judy says, "It was memorable for me!"

33

England and Our Last Days in Seattle

The year 1967 was Cliff's last year at the university, but he still had his dissertation to research and complete. Life for me was getting easier. Now our children and one of my day care children were in school. I only had John, one of Olive's children, to care for during the daytime.

During this time, I began to sell Beeline Clothes by holding home parties. I would only do one or two parties a week. One benefit of doing this was that I could purchase samples at a fraction of the retail price. I purchased more of them in my size, so when the season was over, some of them went into my wardrobe! I enjoyed doing the parties. It was a diversion and an opportunity to meet with other people, but it was no booming business.

During our years both in Spokane and Seattle, we would take trips back home to visit Cliff's family and Frieda and some of our other relatives. Usually, we would be gone for two to three weeks during the summer. Along the way, we would visit more friends and relatives. We hardly ever stayed in motels or hotels. Our favorite and mostly the only restaurant was McDonalds. The kids loved McDonalds. When we came to a town and a McDonalds sign was visible, they would shout, "McDonalds!"

During our time in Seattle, we had a lot of out-of-town guests. Brother Otto came frequently, and sister Ann and Rudy came twice.

When the World's Fair was on in Seattle, a good number of other relatives and friends also came. We enjoyed showing them around our beautiful city too.

For Cliff, his dissertation was looming in his face. He still had quite a lot of the research to do before he could complete it. A dissertation had to be based on research in original primary materials. The documents being researched had to be produced mostly by the people who were participants in the topic being researched. It could not be based on published books, although one was expected to be thoroughly familiar with what had already been published regarding the subject. It had to make very clear how the research advanced knowledge about the topic.

One's dissertation also was to be written in the person's major field of study. Cliff's was modern German history. Noticing that controversy existed as to why Germany did not develop an effective jet fighter earlier during World War II, Cliff decided to do his dissertation on that topic. It would involve researching the policies of the German aircraft and manufacturers of aircraft engines as well as the records of Hitler's government and the German defense department at the time. To accomplish this research, Cliff needed to go to the Imperial War Museum in London, England, where the pertinent documents were at that time. They had been captured from the Germans at the end of WWII and brought there.

The material that he would research in the War Museum was basically in German. When I think of it, I feel faint. What a task! How could he even have thought of tackling such a horrendous task?

Somehow, we had enough money for him to take off for England and do it. He left on New Year's Day of 1968. The plan was for him to spend three months there. I could spend fifty pages writing about his experiences there, but suffice it to say, he made great progress. However, when the three months were up, he needed more time and more money. He wrote to me for more money. I wrote back and said, "Where should I get the money from? Why don't you contact your adviser, Dr. Emerson, at the university?" He did, and the university sent him some. We think it might have been $1,500. That enabled him to stay another month and a half and complete his research.

While Cliff was gone, I tried to keep the kids occupied. One thing we did was to go to the library each week and pick up some books. I would encourage them to write to their daddy to tell him how many they had read. They enjoyed the plan. Olive and I became even closer friends. She and I did a lot of things together with the kids. We enrolled them in a week-long seminar to enhance their self-confidence and also took them to swimming lessons.

Olive and I also both received an invitation for a free dinner at a classy restaurant just for listening to a presentation regarding land acquisition opportunities in the southern USA. Just for fun, we decided to go. It was an opportunity to purchase a lot in a supposedly thriving new residential development in New Mexico. Olive decided to purchase one. I thought if she could, why not me? After all, Cliff would soon have a great job, and it was only $29 per month. We could afford that. So I did too. We laughed about it then and have many times since. I still have that land. I pay $5 a year in taxes!

We did visit the site on one of our vacations. It is a flat piece of grassland with mountains in the distance and is about four miles south of Belen. When I purchased it, it was supposed to be absorbed "momentarily" as a suburb of fast-growing Belen! One of the reasons the taxes are so low on it today is because it is being utilized as pastureland. We are giving the land to one of our children!

While Cliff was still in England, he also sent out applications for a teaching position at various universities. He received three promising inquiries. One was from the University of Idaho in Boise. Another was from the University of Manitoba in Winnipeg, and the third was from Northern Michigan University (NMU) in Marquette, Michigan. One of Northern's history professors, Stephen Barnwell, knew Scott Littel at the University of Washington. Barnwell had once taught there briefly. When Barnwell learned that Littel had recommended Cliff, it is said that he said to the rest of the history department, "That's good enough for me. If Littel has recommended Cliff, I recommend him to the department."

The department, in turn, recommended him to Northern's administration, and it offered Cliff the job without an in-person interview. Cliff accepted the position as a history instructor while he was still in England. His salary, without his dissertation yet written, was going to be only $8,500 annually. Even then, that was low. It certainly would not make us prosperous as I had fancied at times. However, that did not seem to matter just then. It sounded promising for the future, and it would be the beginning of a different and new kind of life for us all.

34

Goodbye, Seattle: Marquette, Here We Come!

Cliff returned, and the kids were ecstatic to see their daddy again. It was great to finally have him back again.

The task now was to get ready for our next move. We placed an advertisement into the paper to sell the house. It sold very quickly, and we were allowed to remain in it until August. We were especially delighted to have made a $4,000 profit. We had never had that much money in our lives before. The experience also caused us to be sensitized to how, in the right circumstances, money could be made through real estate. It was something we did not forget and would utilize later.

Cliff worked again during the summer. To make our trip to Marquette a special camping vacation, we purchased a twelve-by-twelve-foot tent, sleeping bags, air mattresses, and a gas lantern. This was the first time in our thirteen years of marriage, except for purchasing cars, that we spent more than $50 on anything. It was such a thrill to be free to be able to do that. We were careful with our spending, though, because we wanted to preserve the $4,000 for a down payment on a home in Marquette.

Before we left, we made a trial-run weekend camping trip. Everyone loved it. Our thinking was that when we got to Marquette, we would just live in our tent until we were able to purchase a home.

Oh, yes, and before we left Seattle, I had Cliff purchase a couple of good quality suits in which to begin his teaching career.

We again rented a small U-Haul trailer and packed it to the maximum with all of our belongings that we could possibly get into it. We didn't take any furniture or beds. After we had to vacate our house, in order to get everything finalized, we stayed at Olive's a few more days. Then, after some tearful and heart-wrenching goodbyes to our good friends, especially Olive and her children, we hooked the trailer to our old Plymouth and took off for a leisurely trip to Marquette.

We enjoyed the camping, building bonfires, barbecuing, and the many new scenes and attractions we came upon as we went, etc. Once, when we went to a restaurant for breakfast (not a usual thing), the waitress asked what we wanted to eat. Our little Mark instantly piped up without a moment's hesitation and shouted, "Hamburger!"

After 1,915 miles of travel, and without any breakdowns (thank you, Lord), we approached Marquette on M28 from the high terrain just west of the city. But where was the city? All we could see from there was a huge body of water. It looked like we were approaching an ocean. Of course, it was Lake Superior, the lake we would come to respect like no other and to some degree also love. But where was Marquette? When we finally got down into it, compared to the big cities we had become accustomed to, we were surprised at its size. Truthfully, we were somewhat disappointed, although not too greatly, and certainly nothing like my mom once was when she first arrived in Canada as you may recall from chapter 2.

In time, too, it "grew on us," and we came to love it more and more and now have even chosen to retire in it. We found that it had many benefits. No long traffic lines, beautiful beaches close at hand, a nice ski hill, wilderness with small lakes and rivers nearby, and many of the benefits of having four seasons without the extremes that sometimes go with them.

Upon our arrival, we immediately looked for its campground and soon set up camp at Marquette's Tourist Park. We then scouted out the town and drove through the university's grounds—a lot of red brick buildings. There were also a couple of administrative/classroom buildings that were truly of an outstanding classic Gothic architectural style. They reminded us of some of those at the University of Washington, and that helped Cliff, especially, to feel a little more at home in this new university setting.

Classes began shortly. So out of our tent emerged Cliff on that special first day of classes, all dressed up in one of his classy new suits. As he passed professors coming and going, he noticed that almost all of them were dressed rather casually. How come? It was clear that at this university, almost all the professors dressed much more casually than they generally did at the University of Washington. Consequently, one of the first things Cliff felt he needed to do was to buy some more casual clothes! We have often laughed about that unexpected "culture shock." It soon became clear to all of us that Michigan's Upper Peninsula ("the UP") in general was not nearly as much into fancy dressing as some parts of America. Our family came to love that too, although not me so much. I have always enjoyed getting dressed up for special occasions. Cliff never came near to wearing out those two expensive suits.

Cliff had no more than nicely gotten started with teaching when it began to pour for three days at least! Pretty much everything got soaking wet. We just had to find different housing! Before we made any moves, two of Cliff's future colleagues, history professors Richard Sonderreger and Robert McClellan, showed up at our tent entrance to see how we were doing. It was very thoughtful of them to do that. Seeing the untenable situation we were in—our tent was literally sitting in water—McClellan invited us to move into the unused third floor of his house. What a welcome invitation! We not only had the use of that third floor, but he and his wife, Sarah, invited us to join them for the evening meal all the while we were there. They also treated our children as equal with their four, about the same ages as ours. They took us on some outings and showed us some of the special places to "hang out" like Little Presque Isle.

Of course, we immediately began looking for a house. Believe it or not, there were only three homes for sale in Marquette at the time. We decided on an older one located at 325 W. College Avenue. It had lots of space—three stories—but the lot was only fifty-by-fifty square feet and was on the corner of a busy street with stoplights right in front of the house. We didn't like the location, but the other two homes were too small to meet our needs.

We went to the bank with our $4,000 and with what we thought was a great credit record.

The banker turned us down flat! Why?

"Because," he said, "you have no credit!"

I became quite upset and said, "But we have never charged anything and have no debts. Why don't we have good credit? Furthermore, my husband has a job as a professor at Northern."

He said, "That's the problem." He went on to explain how a person creates a good credit record. I began to cry.

The bank manager noticed what was happening and asked, "What's the matter?"

We told him the story, and he immediately granted us the loan! It would take three weeks before we could take possession of the house. The McClellan's allowed us to stay all of that time and, in a sense, be part of their family.

While at the McClellans, I enrolled our kids in Sandy Knoll, a nice elementary school within walking distance both from the McClellans and the house we had just purchased.

Meanwhile, Cliff was well into his teaching. He asked me to help him by typing his syllabi, handouts, tests, etc. While the kids were in school, I helped Sarah wherever I could. I cleaned, helped her with projects, and helped with the cooking.

Initially, I did not think of being employed in any way outside of the home. Cliff was now a professor; I didn't need to go to work! I wanted to be home when my children got home from school. I didn't want them to come home to an empty house. Initially, going to work wasn't on my radar.

As soon as our house became available, we got our stuff out of storage and began moving in. We scouted around for used furniture. We did buy a new couch! The kids loved the house. Mark and Virgil shared a room, and Fern had her own room, an unusually long one. Her father set up his office in one end of it too. Understandably, she didn't particularly like that. I don't remember why he didn't use the third floor.

The whole third floor wasn't used. The kids could use it in any way they wanted to. I, however, was never very happy with the place. I didn't like the fact that it was on a corner lot where we heard the noisy traffic stop and go in the early hours of the morning, had almost no yard, and had no bathroom on the main floor; but it was home and it was ours. We wouldn't just be paying rent, and we would be building some equity. We remembered how that had paid off in Seattle.

The kids settled into the neighborhood very quickly. Fern made loyal lifetime friends with Sue Anderson and Julie Ellsworth. Virgil and Mark also found friends in the neighborhood right close to our house, and later with the Lynches and the Makis, their dear friends to this day.

The kids loved playing up on the third floor of the house. On one mild spring day while playing with a ball, someone missed it, and it went through the open window. It landed on the snow on the roof of that second floor. The ball was too far down to be able to reach it from inside the house. No problem. Virgil, never afraid of trying anything once, climbed out the window and went down the somewhat slushy wet snowy roof to retrieve it. Suddenly, he slipped, and over the edge he went, landing on the roof of the first-floor porch and then kept right on going onto a snow pile on the edge of the sidewalk. It was fortunate that he landed on that, then slid off of it right onto the sidewalk. Whew! Wow!

Just then, two priests were walking along that sidewalk, and Virgil slid onto it right in front of them. How providential! Virgil was not hurt. Had he been, how nice it would have been to have a couple of caring priests right there to help him. Virgil jumped right up, brushed himself off, smiled sheepishly, and assured the priests that he was okay. They, nonetheless, brought him into the house and told us what had happened, very happy that they had not just witnessed a terrible accident. Everyone had a good laugh before the grateful priests continued on their way.

Speaking of Virgil's encounters with priests, in Seattle, he and his siblings somehow snuck out the front of our house and attempted to cross the street in front of a Volkswagen. It was being driven by a priest. The car actually just missed him, and a priest again brought him into the house and explained. Years later, Virgil's comment was, "Tough way to meet priests!"

Soon, too, for that postage-stamp-sized lot, we purchased an above-ground twelve feet in diameter by three feet deep pool and set it up in the little bit of space there was by the driveway. That was a summer highlight for the kids along with such things as playing Kick the Can with the neighbor kids. During the winter, the kids made a little ice rink in that little side yard and played hockey. Fern was the goalie, and the boys drafted enough kids to create a couple of small teams.

35

Getting the Children Involved in Marquette

We were interested in giving our children every opportunity we could for them to develop into mature, competent, well-rounded young people with views and values that we felt were important for them to have in life. That—for me, at least—at this point in our lives included religious instruction.

There were several other things I pretty much assumed primary responsibility for. One of the first things was to try to make musicians out of our children. I enrolled them in Suzuki violin lessons. We ordered a tiny violin for Mark and found a regular-sized one for Virgil and Fern. They, especially Virgil, were doing rather well. Their teacher really drilled them on pieces, like "Twinkle, Twinkle, Little Star." Then some kids at school began teasing them about playing the violin and playing pieces like that, and our kids lost interest.

We then purchased a used piano. The kids took lessons for a couple of years, but then that too fizzled out. Fern, however, did play the flute. She began in Seattle in her fourth grade and continued through high school. She will be the first to admit that because she was in the marching band, she could avoid gym class practices which were uncomfortable for her. That is as far as my musicians got.

When the weather got colder, we became interested in them learning to ski and skate. The boys wanted to go snowmobiling too. But we felt that skill and pleasure could be acquired later on, so we declined their wishes on that one. I purchased skis and took them to lessons. They loved it and they all became pretty good skiers. I took them skiing almost every Saturday.

Because I took them skiing and either waited for them there or came home and then went back for them, I decided to try the sport too. I went to a rummage sale and found a pair of skis and tried it first on the little bunny hill. Then, I tried a little higher hill. I didn't have much success. One of our neighbors happened to be out on the hill, too, and noticed my skis. She told me that I was trying to do downhill skiing with cross-country skis! Embarrassed, I found some downhill skis. I began doing quite well, even coming down some higher slopes. Fern loved seeing how well I was doing and encouraged me to try an even higher hill. I did, and that turned out to be a disaster. I lost control and came barreling down the hill at breakneck speed. It scared me to death. I fell hard. Thankfully, I didn't get badly hurt. It certainly knocked the wind out of me! That ended my skiing endeavors.

Virgil also had an accident on the slopes. He was coming down a hill on an inner tube and smashed into a pile of logs at the bottom. He tore one of his kidneys and ended up in the hospital for seven days and was supposed to lay low for nine weeks. Thankfully, it healed well. No priests there to save him from harm that time!

I purchased skates for the kids too and got them started on that as well. Mark especially took to hockey, played on teams for several years, often as the goalie, and sometimes was the goalie on travel teams.

I enrolled the boys in Boy Scouts and Fern in 4-H. Fern especially loved that and became a competent seamstress.

I remember that at one of the first Boy Scout meetings, they announced that they were going to have a group dinner, and everyone was asked to bring their own pasties.

I wondered, *What on earth is a pastie?* I soon discovered that it was one of the favorite foods in the UP. It used to be a main food that miners in this area took with them into the mines. It was a recipe that the UP Welch miners brought with them from Wales ("Cousin Jacks," they were called).

36

An Absentee Dad

(I would like to add that Cliff included this title and most of this chapter.) The kind of difficult subject matter Cliff was asked to teach when he first started teaching at Northern Michigan University (and for some time thereafter) was unexpected. That interfered a good deal with the amount of time he was able to help with the children or to spend time with them. It meant—as it had back in Seattle, although now for somewhat different reasons—that I had to take care of many of the children's needs myself.

Why was his teaching assignment so demanding? Ordinarily, a professor would teach in the areas in which he or she had done their in-depth studying while in graduate school. In his case, that was modern European history. Northern had such a course known as Western Civilization since 1500. He was asked to teach one section of that class during his first quarter and during some quarters thereafter. That was just fine. That was exactly what a person with his academic background would expect. Great.

Cliff also was asked to teach two sections of a course that was part of a program called Common Learning. In theory, an instructor teaching such a course was expected to have a comprehensive grasp of all kinds of knowledge concerning a particular large area of the world and period of time. In the broad field of the humanities, which history is in, as opposed to science, for instance, that included a knowledge of such areas as history, philosophy, literature, art, music, politics, religion, science, culture, etc. for a particular period of time.

The instructor was expected to be able to draw on all of these areas of knowledge to show how they were interrelated to create the particular culture of that particular time and area and also to show which of these cultural ideas and practices had endured and were still shaping the culture of that particular area today. It was a very idealistic and daunting program, basically too idealistic to be doable by even an older seasoned professor.

Most of the experienced professors considered such a course too idealistic and demanding and refused to teach it. Being tenured, they could get away with that. Some resigned, however, because of pressure to do so. Cliff, being a new professor, did not realistically have that option. He was asked to teach two sections of this kind of a course during his first quarter and for some years thereafter. The particular class he was asked to teach was called The Medieval and Renaissance World—even though he had never even taken a basic survey course in medieval history. Preparing for such a course and continuing to upgrade it to what it should be would be a daunting task.

Cliff was shocked, and yes, scared, when he learned of his "fate" regarding this. How could he possibly teach that kind of a course well? How could there not be many unhappy students? How could this not jeopardize his job and probably result in his termination? Consequently, preparing for his classes required every minute that he could devote to it.

Up until 1974, his teaching assignments never included an in-depth course in the field in which he had done his major studies.

The student uprising in the fall of 1968 was an additional substantial demand on not only Cliff's time but on that of the entire university community. The uprising required giving considerable time to faculty meetings to plan how to best handle various situations and possibilities.

Then there was the writing of Cliff's dissertation which was also in progress during his early years at Northern. It was due to be defended no later than the summer of 1971. Drafts had to be sent back and forth to his directing professor in Seattle. I typed them. Footnotes at that time still had to be placed at the bottom of the pages to which they applied. Typing this kind of work was stressful and extremely time-consuming.

The dissertation turned out to be 284 pages long. When I think of how easy it is today with the computer, I can hardly believe that I did what needed to be done back then. On a happier note, in connection with it all, going back to Seattle to defend his dissertation was a nice by-product of the effort—a month-long vacation trip for the family. We stayed with Olive for a few days again. We visited George Scott, a good friend and fellow graduate student. He also attended Cliff's defense of his dissertation.

One of the areas in which Cliff could have been more involved in the kids' lives was their spiritual development. When we moved to a new area, our priority had always been to find a good church. In this case, however, with Cliff having come to question the reliability of the Bible, his new views had a decisive impact on what kind of a church he would agree to attend in the future.

It turned out that the head of the history department who had hired Cliff was a Presbyterian. Knowing that Cliff had gone to a Presbyterian College, he invited him to the Presbyterian church that he was attending. We went, and following that, Cliff said, "This is the only church I will attend." He sensed that it was a church that would not put any pressure on him about the views he now had. I was not happy with the choice from the start.

As time went on, I became even more concerned. We would hear from the pulpit that baptism is the rite of entry into heaven. Later, at a funeral, we heard, "This person was baptized as an infant, so we know he is in heaven." You will recall from my earlier experience that I believed that the Bible teaches that we are saved by faith alone, not through works. Baptism has to be done by someone, so it is a form of work. My question was, if we could be saved by being baptized, why did Christ need to come and die for us?

Despite the reservations I had about the doctrines of the church, all of us found the people of the church very congenial, helpful, and gracious.

Cliff kept his promise to attend this particular church with us, although he didn't want me to broadcast the fact that he had come to have doubts about the reliability of the Bible. I felt it was better for the children to see him go to church with us than for me and them to go elsewhere without him. I felt that I could teach them the truth about salvation at home.

Cliff soon made some very good friends at church and began identifying with some of the church's needs. One day, the pastor appeared at our home to ask Cliff if he would join the session, the governing body of the church. Cliff, with some reservations, agreed to do so. Even though while he was being asked, I interjected, "But he doesn't even believe. He has doubts."

The pastor's response was, "Oh, we all have doubts. It's good that he is honest about them."

Cliff decided to join mainly for social reasons and to be helpful, not that he cared that much anymore about the doctrinal positions that the church held.

37

Becoming Financially Independent

When it came to paying the bills, I soon discovered that Cliff's checks didn't stretch far enough. We had to watch every penny we spent. Everything we purchased for the kid's sports was secondhand. By the end of the month, there was no money left. Cliff mentioned to me that there was an opening for a secretarial position in the history department. It would be secretary for all the members of the department. I immediately said, "No thanks." Can you imagine the stress it could be trying to be secretary to nine professors? One not knowing what the other ones had given you to do? Going to work again had no appeal for me.

Finally, in the spring of 1969, Cliff said to me, "Why don't you give Amway another try? I doubt it'll work! But if you wish, give it another try." That was the company that my friend, Vivian, had introduced me to in Seattle. We had both put our signature on the application. Doing Amway appealed to me because I could manage my hours and be home when the children got home. Cliff's negative statement actually motivated me.

I had continued to feel somewhat disheartened during these years. That is because the road Cliff had taken was so different from what we had discussed when we were dating and vastly different from the life that either of us had expected we would live. We expected for it to be in some kind of evangelical Christian ministry. His faith crises and his commitment to his job didn't allow for any options for a turnaround.

I began to feel that Amway could be an option—a ministry, in a sense—through which I could help people financially. I thought of the proverb, "Give people a fish and they will eat for a day. Teach them to fish and they will eat for a lifetime." I truly felt that through Amway, I could be helping people (teaching them to fish) to better their situations. I prayed about it. I went to see some pastors about the possibility of them being supportive of the cause or maybe even becoming involved. One actually signed up for the business. I discovered later that Pastor Charles Stanley was a big Amway distributor. Robert Schuler was a big promoter of it.

My own sponsor, Vivian Strickert, was a missionary and, of course, was a Christian. My upline sponsors were also. I learned that the founders of the company, Rich DeVos and Jay Van Andel, also were. They vigorously promoted the idea of helping people. In fact, I think that a strong motivating factor behind the whole business was that of helping people while also helping one's self. So I felt good about going into the business seriously.

To begin, however, I needed some money. I went to the bank and got a signature loan of $1,000. They readily gave it to me. I ordered the basic products and a few starter kits. I set a goal to reach the top level of the refund schedule in the first month. I contacted a few people to sell the products and also to try to get some distributors involved. Soon, I had a little group of distributors. I immediately began holding weekly training meetings on Thursday nights to train in selling techniques and to provide information about the products. I had a second weekly meeting on Tuesdays to recruit new distributors and encouraged distributors to bring friends—prospects—to hear the sales plan. Soon, our little group grew to quite a number of distributors.

I offered my help to show the plan to any distributor who had a prospect that wasn't available on Tuesdays or Thursdays or both. I encouraged a new distributor to invite friends into their home, and I would go there and present the plan. In this way, these new distributors could speed up their progress of getting distributors under them and also begin to acquire some clients. The sales volume produced by their distributors would be added to their total volume and income.

Amway had an awards program for reaching certain sales volumes and for reaching certain levels in the refund schedule. It went from 3 to 25 percent. This was on top of the profit made from retail sales. I promoted this and cheered people on as they reached certain levels. We had fun at our meetings; we were like a social club. In addition to the weekly meetings, I held monthly meetings as well. As the business grew, we would sometimes plan a weekend at a hotel for training purposes and for just some fun and relaxation. At these events, we would plan a worship service for Sunday mornings for those who wished to attend. I offered to pay for the weekend for anyone achieving a certain volume.

I use "I" and "we" interchangeably because although I was managing and building the business, Cliff came to play a big role in it too, in some ways. He was impressed with the progress that we were making and began to join me for the larger meetings. He was very helpful in interacting with our distributors at our functions. Each month or more often, we would have a large semitruck bring a load of products to our house. Our driveway was too short to accommodate the big truck without it sticking way out into the street. Cliff or someone else would direct traffic around the end of the truck as it was being unloaded into our basement. The whole family, especially our boys, and sometimes their friends, would be involved in carrying cases of products down into our basement.

I reached my goal the first month, and I made about $1.000. The next major goal was to do that consecutively for three months. I did and was awarded a free three-day trip to the home office in Ada, Michigan. We were put up in the Pantlind Hotel (later Amway Grand Hotel) in Grand Rapids. A little later, I doubled my volume for a couple of months. When I think back on this achievement, I feel that the Lord was really blessing the whole endeavor.

I tried hard to help people who were struggling financially. Often, I would give the starter kits to prospective distributors for free if they couldn't afford it. I went out of my way to help them.

However, unfortunately, not many in this category did what was necessary to become a success in the business.

In addition to holding a lot of meetings, I sold a fair number of products to my own clients on the retail level. I also sent out a monthly newsletter that promoted new products and recognized distributors for their accomplishments. Our children were my secretaries in getting the newsletters folded and stamped. Recently, one of their friends laughed as he shared with me how he used to help our kids get the newsletters ready because they weren't allowed to go and play with their friends until the job was done. The kids always were a great help, too, in getting the house prepared for the many meetings I held in our home—although sometimes quite reluctantly! Fern quite regularly made brownies for me for the meetings. It also wasn't long until I hired a part-time secretary to help with the book work involved in operating our organization.

When one of my distributors, Marge, reached the top of the refund schedule for three consecutive months, I awarded her with a trip to Hawaii to attend Jim Janz's seminar there. Jim was my up-line sponsor. He awarded me the free trip to that seminar also. Marge and I stayed there for three weeks, even though the seminar was only for a few days. Another year, Jim awarded me a free trip to his seminar in British Columbia.

Sometimes, I went to help distributors in places like San Jose, Seattle, and Lansing. I had distributors in such areas because I had sponsored them at one time here, and they moved there from Marquette. My sponsor, Vivian Strickert, sponsored my distributor in San Jose for me. She was a real go-getter.

Besides Amway improving our financial situation, there were other benefits and rewards too. For example, with her permission, I will share part of Bea Wertanen's story. She was a very shy lady when we first met. She answered my ad to come and clean for me. I showed her the Amway business, and she signed up. I had a meeting at her home to help her get started. She began coming to my training and recruiting meetings and soon was bringing prospects. She became one of the top retailers in our group and continued to find people that she wanted me to introduce to the business. I would do that for her. Soon, she had quite an organization under her, and her group became one of the most successful I had.

She had been cleaning for others too; one of them was for a professor. After she was in the business for a while, she told me, "Before I got into Amway, when that professor would come home, I would hide in the bedroom so I wouldn't have to talk to him. Now I can talk to anyone!"

Another couple told me that before they got into Amway, they had planned to end their marriage. Amway changed that.

Another lady said to me, "I can see that church is important to you." She then began attending.

At our meetings, we stressed having a positive attitude. We often used Robert Schuller's creed. I especially liked to emphasize the last phrase:

> When faced with a mountain
> I will not quit!
> I will keep on striving
> I will climb over, find a pass
> through, tunnel underneath—
> or simply stay and turn the
> mountain into a gold mine,
> With God's help!

38

A Diversion

Just before Christmas in the fall of 1972, I got severe chest pains. I had similar pains in Seattle. The doctor there said it was nerves and put me on Valium. When I went to the doctor in Marquette, he said that it was not nerves; it was a gallbladder problem. He referred me to a surgeon who removed both the gallbladder and the appendix. The incision went all the way from my chest to my appendix. They told me that my gallstones were the largest they had ever seen. A nurse asked me if they could put one of them into their display case. My recuperation time would take a while.

Fern was now a big help, but for a while, she would ask to go to the Andersons after school pretty much every day. Mrs. Bill Anderson was her 4-H leader. I let her go for a while but told her to be home to help with supper.

She asked to go over there night after night when I really needed her to help me. I finally said, "This is ridiculous."

Then, just before Christmas, after school, she called and said that she was over at the Andersons and said that she would be home to help with dinner. I was upset.

Christmas day came, and when it came time to open gifts, the kids all wanted me to be the first one to open a gift.

I said, "No, I want you kids to open one first." They insisted. Fern handed me a nicely wrapped gift. It was a beautiful professionally folded blazer.

Fern said, "I made it."

I said, "You didn't."

"Try it on."

It was done beautifully. At first, I was afraid to try it on because when I made things for myself, I always had to make several adjustments. How could this possibly fit without it having been tried on while in the process? I did, and it fit perfectly!

I took her into my arms and squeezed her and said, "Fern, you are a wonderful girl. I love you."

Then, with tears in her eyes, she said, "Mom, you know when you got mad at me for going over to the Andersons?"

I felt so bad for being upset with her and gave her another hug.

During those years, despite the fact that I was heavily involved in the Amway business, I was also very involved at the church. I taught Sunday School to the seventh and eighth graders. Our kids went through my class. It soon grew to where the minister split it into two sections.

During the early and mid-seventies, I became chairperson of the church's Christian Education Committee. I discovered a report of our committee in my files and was surprised to recall how active the committee was. We held teacher training meetings and invited other churches to join us, reviewed and updated the various curricula, obtained more teaching aids for the teachers, organized social activities for families, began family enrichment classes, organized distribution of food to the needy, and so on.

I got the children involved as much as possible in the church's activities for children and youth. I enrolled them in its Vacation Bible School each year. The church also had a camp ministry at Presbytery Point on Lake Michigamme. I sent them there each year for a week-long camp. The mornings were taken up with Bible lessons and singing, and the afternoons were fun times with lots of games, swimming, hiking, learning how to canoe, and other interesting options. In the evenings, they would sit around a big bonfire and sing and share. They especially enjoyed going down the Sturgeon River, over its rapids, and sometimes over its challenging waterfall. They always made great friends over the week and enjoyed being pen pals for a time.

39

Discovering a Great Building Site

The Amway business grew more quickly than we ever imagined. One of the first things we did was buy a new car. It was an eight passenger Oldsmobile Custom Cruiser Wagon. It felt like riding in a hovercraft compared to the rusty little old Plymouth we had up until that time. Our kids loved our new car.

We outgrew our lot and house. It was not set up to handle a large number of products and had no parking for people coming to meetings, etc. We had to find a place where ten to fifteen cars could be parked without bothering the neighbors. It quickly became evident that we would need to build.

In 1971, we began to search for a lot. On the west edge of town, we found a five-acre piece of land which initially looked like it would work. It had a fairly deep gully along the front of it and had no water or sewer or road into it. It was very reasonably priced—only $5,000. As we watched the road being built in front of it, we discovered another piece of flat land just west of where the road being built ended. It was part of a street right-of-way that extended west into such a deep ravine that it was clear that continuing the street beyond that flat piece of land would never happen. A cul-de-sac could be developed in front of it as well. The site had large rock outcroppings about forty feet high on either side of it. The flat area was large enough for a generous building site and yard. A beautiful creek ran through that deep ravine at the back of the property.

It immediately struck both Cliff and I. "What an ideal building site that would be. That is the site that we would really like." Acquisition of the site, however, was quite complicated. However, that it happened at all seems miraculous. I think God had his hand in it.

We called the owner. He instantaneously said, "No."

We decided to go and see him in person; he might be more amenable that way and be willing to sell.

Before we went, I sat on a rock on that property and prayed, "Lord, if you give us this land, we will use it for you." Of course, for that to happen, Cliff's heart would have to be changed.

We found the old gentleman who owned the land hoeing his garden. We befriended him a bit, and he softened up.

"Well," he said, "I will have to ask my kids."

He did. They had no objection to him selling the land.

"But I will have to ask you for a good price!" he warned. It turned out to be very reasonable.

The site extended as far west as the creek and included the south rock outcropping to just over its crest. North of this property was an east to west property line and was the additional flat area we needed for an adequate-sized building site. Eastward, these properties went as far as another property line going north and south. That was the boundary line between the City of Marquette and Marquette Township. The property we desired and needed—a little more than an acre—was owned or controlled by four different parties. One being the gentleman from whom we had already purchased a parcel, and another owned the property in the township to the north of the east-west property line. Another piece was a lot in the city just east of the north-south city/township boundary line. The city agreed to vacate a piece of street right of way just east of the city/township boundary line where its city street ends. It took us three months to acquire all of these properties.

All in all, it cost $8,500 for these pieces of property. Because of Amway, we had the money to cover these costs. There were no water and sewer lines or road into it. That would cost $26,000.

That included a cul-de-sac in the front of our house that measured about one-hundred and twenty feet across. We were able to more than defray that cost by dividing the front part of the five-acre parcel of land that we had purchased at the beginning of this process into four lots and selling them.

40

Our Dream Home

We looked at a lot of house plans. The house had to have a large living room in order to be able to seat about thirty people for Amway meetings. We wanted it to be a wraparound L-shaped one-story structure with big glass sliding doors facing the west and south of the living room and of the master and guest bedrooms. It had to have plenty of room for the family and a full basement. We wanted a room for servicing Amway distributors that was separate from the house's main living quarters with easy access from the street.

We shared our ideas with an architect. He brought us a plan that ignored pretty much everything we had suggested to him. It was a standard cookie-cutter plan. He said that we couldn't have a house with all of those windows in our northern part of the country. By that time, we had secured a reputable builder, Al Harden, and told him what the architect said. I drew up a rough sketch of what we wished to have. He basically said, "Give me the dimensions of the house, and I can build all those things into it."

To leave enough space behind the west side of the house for a good-sized yard, we had the house built so far to the east that the garage and Amway room and two feet of the eastern wall of the house were in the city. The rest of it was in Marquette Township. That meant that we would be paying taxes on the house to the township and the city. It, nevertheless, was a good decision. It helped us achieve our purposes.

We took out a loan to build our house. Construction began in August 1972. Our builder consulted with us frequently, made a few great suggestions, and did a great job in general, especially on the floor to ceiling fireplace. For it, the kids and Cliff and I gathered different types of beautiful local rocks in addition to the ones that the builder contributed.

We moved into our new home in February 1973.

Our dream home

When we built, the natural gas lines were not yet in our area, so we chose electricity for our heating system. It was quite reasonable initially.

The house without the garage was over 3,000 square feet. We were all very delighted with it.

My Family: Mark, Fern, Virgil, me, and Cliff

The kids all had their own rooms and their own bathroom. Cliff and I had our own offices. There was a special room adjacent to the garage just for Amway products. The living and family rooms accommodated the numerous meetings I would hold in them. Jim Janz, our up-line Amway sponsor, visited us once from Vancouver, British Columbia, did an Amway meeting for us, and was so happy to see what Amway had helped us acquire.

Outside, it felt like we were in a camp setting. Those high rock outcroppings on either side of us and the deep creek ravine and high rock outcropping on the other side of it gave us a lot of privacy. No one could build beside or behind us. Then there were the ten acres of rugged undeveloped land adjacent to our property—although not ours—through which we could roam freely.

One of our very first experiences at our new home was when our son, Mark, invited a friend to visit. He had a BB gun. They went out onto the property, and Mark accidentally shot a BB pellet into one of his big toes. I rushed him to the emergency room. They removed the pellet, and we returned home.

Shortly thereafter, a policeman showed up at our door. He said, "I understand there has been a shooting here. It is unlawful to shoot a gun in the city of Marquette."

To this, I quickly responded, "We are not in the city. We are in Marquette Township."

He was nonplussed, I think, turned around, and left!

This was the first time that we had benefited so explicitly from our house being built on the city/township property line!

During these same years, Cliff was becoming more rather than less confirmed about his doubts and lack of faith. I used to say grace before meals. Sometimes, however, he would make negative comments about the practice in the presence of the kids.

Rather than exposing them to any more of that than I could help, I quit doing it. I was careful not to bring up the subject of religion of any kind in their presence. He came to feel more and more that he didn't want the children to be taught that the Bible is true. He wanted to spare them from, perhaps, having to go through the same shattering experience later on as he did on finding that perhaps it was not true or reliable. Better, he thought, to just let them draw their own conclusions from what they would hear and observe as they grew up.

He told me at times how sorry he felt for all those people in church who were so duped. He began finding more and more excuses as to why he didn't have time to go to church. He came to feel that he didn't want me to "waste" my time doing things at church. Nonetheless, he continued to let me be involved and never tried to prevent it.

41

A Huge Disappointment

As far as the new house was concerned, all went well until the huge amount of snow that came during the winter of 1973 and melted rather quickly, and then a heavy rainstorm came at the same time. Our basement flooded. Why? Our excellent builder thought that because the house was sitting rather high on sand and because a ravine into which water could drain was close by, drain tile along the foundations of the house would not be necessary.

We called the builder, and he immediately had a backhoe here to dig a trench around the south and west side of the house deep enough to lay the drain tile below the level of the house's footings.

What a job. We were "tree huggers" at the time. We had saved almost all of the trees in the backyard. That made it difficult for the backhoe to get to where it needed to be to work efficiently. Once dug, the bottom of the trenches first needed to be filled with six inches of coarse gravel which had to be wheelbarrowed in on a rickety plank scaffolding built into the sides of the piles of dirt. It took a lot of strength and skill to manage wheelbarrows full of gravel (or even half full) on such scaffolding. The drainage pipes had to be laid on top of the gravel. A good deal of the dirt just had to be shoveled back into them.

The north side of the house needed a similar treatment. However, the situation was somewhat different and even more difficult. There was only about a six-foot space between the house and the rock outcropping. That meant that there wasn't enough room for a backhoe to get in there. So that trench had to be dug by hand. My hardworking husband and sons again worked tirelessly to get that dirt out. Because of the limited space on which to pile the dirt, the piles got very high quickly. The dirt that still had to come out of the trench had to be thrown higher and higher to get it over the rest of it. Sometimes, as hard as a person heaved a shovel of dirt, it wouldn't make it over the crest of the pile of dirt and would come slithering down again. It was maddening for them at times. It was hard to watch.

Then there was the issue again of how to get the gravel down into and along that long sixty-foot trench. The drain pipe was relatively easy to lay, but then shoveling all that dirt back into the trench was another story. It had to be done very carefully so that the fill going within two feet of the basement wall was only sand, not clay. If clay was placed right next to the basement wall, there was the danger that frost might collapse the wall. All of these measures, while difficult, permanently solved the water problem in the basement.

Doing that trench work was the hardest work Cliff, Virgil, and Mark did in connection with getting our place in shape. The boys did not like it, but it had to be done, so they rose to the challenge.

Though we hired a professional to do a lot of the original landscaping, there was still a lot of other kinds of work that the whole family was involved in doing, like clearing out and burning the small brush, planting shrubs and flowers, etc.

Cliff and the boys also built a beautiful flower rock garden on the north side of the cul-de-sac at the front of the house. There were plenty of rocks on the property to do all kinds of rock work.

About 1975, Cliff decided that he would like to have a vegetable garden. The farmer in him was coming out! To save the flat space in the backyard for a volleyball court, he decided to create a garden by building a three-to-four-foot-high rock wall along the edge of the rock outcropping extending west toward the ravine on the north side of the house.

Then he filled the cavity he created behind it with dirt. Next to the trench work, this was undoubtedly some of the hardest work that Cliff and the boys did. Cliff's dad just happened to be visiting us when this project was launched. He helped put down some of the first rocks for the wall. For that reason, Cliff likes to think of that wall as Fritz's wall and Virgil and Mark's wall, too, and maybe a little of his as well. While a good part of it was completed within a couple of years, some of it has been a work in progress up until the present time (2021). Since launching it, that garden has provided us with years of pleasure and a lot of great vegetables, especially tomatoes, lettuce, cucumbers, and raspberries.

Sometimes the kids would complain and say that their friends didn't have to work like this. It is true, but the work was only in spurts. It surely revealed the kind of stamina my husband and our obedient children had. The boys still sort of wince when they think of that trench-digging experience. They all worked like troopers. The kids learned to do all kinds of things. They also learned to be resourceful, capable, and not afraid to tackle almost anything within reason. It is interesting to see that even now, in 2021, how they often do a lot of things themselves that they could have hired someone else to do. Fern has developed the same kind of traits, although in different circumstances.

An interesting development happened when Mark had a phone interview for the job he now still has. He was asked, "What makes you different from your friends?"

Proudly and without any hesitation, Mark replied, "My parents believed in the work ethic." Both he and we have often laughed about that.

During those years after we were settled in our home, we also gradually began investing in other real estate. We purchased two rental homes as well as a four-acre parcel of property and acquired three additional lots at a tax sale. We also kept the first house we purchased in Marquette as a rental property for a couple of years. This meant that we were paying five mortgages. The rental income pretty much covered three of them. The rental properties, of course, required some renovation, refurbishing, and cleaning from time to time. While the boys were still home, they often helped their dad with some of that too. Fern helped me with the traditional women's work, although there were times when she and I also worked outside of the house. That is how our families raised us, and that's how our family then often worked together too.

Grandpa Cliff having fun teaching our work ethic to Jack and Emma!

42

Happenings with Our Vehicles

Our children were delighted with our Oldsmobile Custom Cruiser Wagon and were happy when we allowed them to take it for a drive. On one occasion, Virgil, then a new driver, took it out right after a fresh snowstorm. We were told the following story years later! He decided to pass a car. He was driving so fast, trying to pass that our car actually was airborne for several feet before it landed in the ditch, full of snow. It had to be pulled out by a wrecker. However, there was no visible damage to the car and, fortunately, no one got hurt!

In about 1974, we splurged and purchased a motorhome and a fourteen-foot motorboat. The kids loved to go on trips with us in that motorhome. I remember on our first trip with it, Mark, then about twelve years old, sat at the table in it with both elbows on the table and a big smile on his face and said, "This is the way to travel!"

To speak of it being the way to travel, one weekend, Cliff and I went out of town, and we left our teenagers—aged fourteen, sixteen, and eighteen—at home. The next day after we returned, a policeman knocked on our door. Mark answered the door and then disappeared! The policeman informed us that a motorhome had been involved in a hit-and-run accident, and it appeared like the motor home was ours. Cliff and I went out with the policeman to see why he thought that. Sure enough, there were paint scratches on the motorhome that looked very suspicious. We called out Virgil and said in anger, "You took the motorhome?"

He said, "Not me!"

Then I called out, "Mark!"

He concurred. The policeman must have been humored by it all. He never gave us a ticket. The person whose car was involved was an attorney. We never heard from him either. Mark was grounded for a month.

The longest trips that we took with the motorhome were going to Canada to visit Cliff's dad and stepmom, my sisters, Frieda and Ann, and other relatives in the area. We took our time going and coming and enjoyed launching the boat on a lake here and there. The kids loved the boat. Virgil and Mark loved being the boat captains.

Mark, Virgil, Grandpa Fritz, and Cliff with our boat

When Cliff felt too busy with his teaching responsibilities, the kids and I would take the outfit and go to Lake Michigamme or Lake Independence for weekends. The boys became very capable in handling the boat and were both cautious and careful with it. They got so we would even let them take it out on Lake Superior by themselves in the right circumstances.

One time, I invited a number of people to go with me in the motorhome to a Church Synod weekend retreat. After that, I was invited to be a member of the Church Synod Committee that met periodically in various states. Another fellow and I became the leaders of one of those retreats for two consecutive years.

43

The Children's Later Years

The kids finished high school from 1976 to 1980. In their latter high school years, they all got jobs in the restaurant industry.

Fern worked as a waitress at the upscale Northwoods Supper Club. She loved waitressing, especially because of the nice tips she sometimes received! Virgil worked at Big Al's as a cook. Mark also worked at Northwoods and a few other places. Later, during his college years, he and a friend established their own tree-trimming business. I was proud to see that all our children were competent and dependable at whatever they chose to do.

Three weeks after Fern graduated from high school, she enrolled in a one-year course at the Patricia Stevens (PS) Career and Finishing School in Milwaukee, Wisconsin. While there, she waitressed at a high-end restaurant, Nantucket Shores. In some ways, she loved it, but she asked herself, "Do I really want to be a waitress all my life?"

The answer was no.

She took a college aptitude test. It suggested production management. She enrolled in the Milwaukee School of Engineering and also got a job with the Square D Manufacturing Company there. The person sitting across the desk from her was Larry Wasicek. They decided to go to San Jose, California, to find jobs there. Fern found a job at Seagate, a computer hard drive manufacturing company; and Larry was at Advanced Cardiovascular Systems, a medical device company, focused then on heart catheter development.

In 1989, Fern married Larry. They returned to Milwaukee for the wedding. It was where Larry's family lived. They had their beautiful wedding in a local church, and their grand wedding reception was in the beautiful Nantucket Shores Restaurant where she had waitressed some years earlier. The setting was extraordinary.

Fern's wedding: Virgil, Mark, Larry, Fern, me, and Cliff

What a special beautiful bride she was. I was so proud of her. Someone asked Larry, "How did you find such a beautiful bride?"

My two sisters, Ann and Frieda, came down from Canada to be at her wedding. They always remembered it fondly.

Both Fern and Larry finished their bachelor's degrees by taking evening classes for years while holding down their professional jobs in California. Both of them were very accomplished in their work. Fern had a knack for creating positions for herself by spotting and filling needs in customer quality roles that involved frequent international travel and negotiating solutions between customers and her internal upper-level management. Larry developed balloon angioplasty catheters and neuro stents resulting in thirty-four patents in his name for his companies. He also enrolled in a real estate class and became a broker. They acquired some California rental properties as well as their current home set on a hill overlooking two beautiful valleys and portions of the city below. The remodels of their house have resulted in a beautiful high-end home.

At first, Virgil and Mark didn't want to go to university. In those days—locally, at least—it seemed that people without a university education were doing just as well as those with one. We talked them into at least taking a course in a trade. Virgil decided on a welding course, and Mark took an air-conditioning and refrigeration course. Virgil ended up doing welding jobs in the bellies of huge tanker ships. He soon was asking himself too, "Do I really want to do this the rest of my life?" Again, the answer was no.

Mark and a friend decided that they wanted to try and find jobs in California. Without experience, they couldn't get any in their field. They ended up doing a tar and roofing job. Then, they and another friend, Ted, went to Texas and Oklahoma, seeking work in the oil fields. When that ended, they headed for Florida but couldn't find work there. Mark gave blood to help keep himself afloat. He never called home for money, though. Eventually, he did call and asked if he could come and stay at home and go to the university. Mark had not been a serious student in high school, so I told him that if he came home, he had to really be serious about his studies. He assured me that he would be. He returned and enrolled at Northern, and by the second year, he was on the dean's honor roll! He and a friend, Arnie, studied like troopers. I was really proud of him.

During these college years, Mark did a paper on the savings we could have if we converted our house to hot air/natural gas heat. One day, he said, "'Why don't we change our heating system to gas heat?"

By that time, gas lines had been installed in our area, and our electric heat bills had skyrocketed to over $600 per month during the colder months. We also had been supplementing that heat with wood—cutting, splitting, and burning several full cords of wood a year.

He suggested that we hire a contractor to help lay out the plans and provide us with the materials and that he would then do the work. He did a great job. I was his helper while Cliff was busy with his teaching. The contractor commended him for the great job he did and offered him a job. I was proud of him and had fun working with him.

Soon after Mark started at Northern, Virgil also decided to come home and go to university. They both majored in electronic engineering, and both of them wisely got jobs at NMU, repairing computers while at school. That made a great addition to their resumes. After graduation, Virgil got a job with the Valmet Paper Company in Appleton, Wisconsin, where he did the computer work to install and upgrade massive paper winders at mills across North America, Argentina, Brazil, Venezuela, and Taiwan. He has also made many trips to Finland where his company is headquartered to set up and test the winders before they are shipped to customer sites. He has continued with Valmet until his retirement this year (2021). He had become one of the company's top engineers. We're sure he will be missed.

Mark was hired by the Chicago Research and Trade Company (CRT). While working at CRT, Mark took a position running its IT department in its London office. More to come on that in chapter 49. CRT ultimately was purchased by Bank of America where he worked his way up to an executive management position, responsible for desktop and server engineering for the bank. For three years, Mark has been managing one of the bank's data architect teams responsible for the inventory of the IT assets of the bank worldwide. He was recently promoted to take his boss's position. We are so proud of him.

In 1996, Virgil found a bride, Jennie Dremel, in Appleton, Wisconsin; however, that marriage didn't last. The fact that Virgil's job required him to be away from home for extended periods of time so frequently probably contributed to the problem. Virgil, nevertheless, continued to love and care for Jennie's daughter as if she was his own, and we considered her our granddaughter. More on her later.

44

Switching Fields

By 1974, Cliff's department was beginning to allow him to teach in-depth courses in his field, especially regarding the Nazi period and WWII. He loved that. I was so glad for him. That, too, presented a problem in terms of having time for the family. So many books were being written regarding that subject. To read just reviews of all of them and just to read a rather small fraction of them, recommend the best of them to the library for purchase, and keep his courses based on the latest and best literature required a good deal of time.

In that year, too, another time-absorbing development happened for Cliff. The department decided that it should offer a course in Canadian history. None of the professors had studied that subject. Because Cliff was from Canada, they felt that he was the most qualified to teach it, even though he had never paid that much attention to that subject while living there. Now he became obliged again to divert a considerable amount of time to reading, developing, and teaching another course in an unfamiliar field.

When I think of how Cliff was expected to teach courses at NMU so often in fields that he had not been prepared for, I marvel at how he never complained to me about it. I wasn't even aware of much of this until I started quizzing him about his career while writing this account.

Cliff in his study at home

Meanwhile, by about 1976, Cliff had been at Northern for nearly ten years. That was the time professors with doctorates usually began to be considered for full professorships. To qualify, in addition to a satisfactory teaching record, it required some reading of papers at conferences and doing some additional original research, writing, and publishing. Cliff had already been promoted to assistant and associate professorships. Full professorship would mean better pay and more control and security.

Preparing for his classes in Canadian history caused him to believe that it made a lot of sense for him to switch his future in-depth research from German to Canadian history. He had become interested in the efforts of the farmers in the Canadian Prairies to get a railroad built to the Hudson Bay. This decision, however, resulted in him spending a considerable amount of time during the next two summers in the archives in Saskatchewan, Manitoba, Ottawa, and elsewhere.

Although I had very mixed feelings about him spending that much time away again, it seemed necessary to advance his career, so I very hesitatingly supported him in that too.

In the summer of 1977, on one of our vacation trips to Saskatchewan, we decided just for old time's sake to visit the site where the Two Rivers Bible Institute had once been. We were shocked to see nothing but crumbling foundations where buildings had once stood. Poplar trees about twenty feet tall had grown in and around them. Being a historian, as Cliff viewed this, he thought of all of the history that was being obliterated by those fast-growing saplings. It would all soon be forgotten if something was not done to record what had happened there. Such an admirable group of people had once lived and operated there. If Northern would just allow him to write a history of this place and these people, and if they would agree to accept that toward getting promoted to full professorship, he would love it. He could write a history on why this Bible school and others arose on the prairies in Canada in the late 1920s and 1930s and show how they had influenced the thinking of that part of the country. Northern's Research Projects Evaluation Committee agreed to accept his proposal.

As Cliff expressed his thoughts to me about this next project, it was as though I heard a voice from heaven say, "This is it. This will bring him back to the Lord." I immediately supported him in this effort, although this would again take him away from the family, big-time. It seemed like he was becoming not only an absentee dad but also an absentee husband.

Cliff did part of his research on this project in the summer and the fall semester of 1978 in Saskatchewan. He was able to obtain a sabbatical leave for that fall and was gone for almost that whole time. That meant he would only receive half of his salary, however. He completed the research in the summer of 1979.

As we'll see later, God was answering prayer and orchestrating this whole development of Cliff's switching of fields.

45

"A Changed Man"

Cliff's research for the TRBI history involved interviewing many former administrators, teachers, students, supporters, and founders of the school as well as other people who still remembered the school and its beginnings.

Most of the school's records had been destroyed through the floods and the devastation the school suffered from them as related above in chapter twenty. Cliff, therefore, in a sense, had to reconstruct that history as to who the founders were, what motivated them, how they established the school, who the teachers, staff, and students were, etc. He sought to identify each person in the pictures which survived (and quite a lot of them did). The correspondence in connection with that alone was very time-consuming. We didn't yet have e-mails!

Initially, he had taken on this project as a purely secular endeavor. He didn't reveal his spiritual struggles to the people he was interviewing. They, for the most part, still thought of him as a solid Bible school graduate who was following the Lord devotedly and doing this project because he felt the Lord was leading him to do so. He taped gobs of interviews.

Often, people would pray something like this for him: "Lord, undertake for Cliff and make him a blessing and a great soul-winner."

Cliff would cringe inside and feel like a horrible hypocrite. However, as he listened, he wished that he could believe again like these people did and in the way he himself used to; but he believed that he just couldn't honestly do so with the doubts he had.

One of the things these people were doing in praying with Cliff so confidently was undermining one of his doubts. You will recall one of his first doubts was whether or not we can actually connect with God in prayer or whether we are just imagining that we are. The way these people prayed was convincing Cliff that they were indeed connecting with him and in communion with someone who was real.

One time, Cliff visited a Mr. Snider, now an old man and a former staff member. He kept expressing his contentment, his desire, and his hope of soon being with the Lord.

"What a great day that will be," he said.

Cliff felt in his heart that that was wonderful. He wished he could believe again, but as noted, he just felt he couldn't. He felt he had to be honest. If the time ever came when he could honestly believe again, he would love to do so. Deep down, he doubted that that would ever be the case again.

Cliff would often be invited to spend the night with the people he interviewed. One night, he was invited to stay with Max Baxter who had taken in his sister in earlier years (see chapter 21). In the morning, while Cliff was getting dressed upstairs, downstairs, he heard Max singing to himself the words of an old hymn as he was preparing breakfast. It included the words:

I do believe, I will believe that Jesus died for me.
That on the cross He shed his blood from sin to set me free.

Instantly and powerfully, those words struck a chord in Cliff's mind and heart. In a flash, it dawned on him that what he needed to do was "will" to believe.

Cliff says it was like God, the Holy Spirit, was right there in the room beside him and said, "Cliff, what you need to do is will to believe God. Will to believe that what he says is true, is true. If you do, your doubts will clear up. Don't hold off on believing until all your doubts have been cleared up. Decide to believe in spite of your remaining doubts."

Cliff said that the message was very powerful, very clear. He said that the implication of what God had said to him was that he had elevated his own thinking—his own reasoning above God's—and that was the source of his problem.

Cliff says that when God spoke those words so strongly and so clearly to him—to his heart—he knew that this was his answer. If he wanted to believe again and have that sweet relationship with God that he once had, he had to "will to believe God" again, to accept God for who the Bible says he is.

So, standing right there in the middle of that bedroom upstairs, he just said to God in all sincerity, "Okay, God, if that's what it takes, I believe."

Instantly, that fellowship with God he had once known was back. It felt so good, he said. He said it felt like a great reunion with a precious friend had happened. Feelings of great joy, gratitude, and praise welled up within him. It also was like a light went on, like a confirmation of Jesus's declaration that he is the light. That spiritual darkness that had settled over his soul and mind about spiritual things had lifted.

The Cliff who went up the stairs the night before came down those same stairs the next morning a changed man.

When Cliff came home, we were again in bed and he, with me in his arms around me again, said, "Honey, I have something I want to tell you. I believe again. I have come back to the Lord!" He then shared with me his experiences that are related in the above paragraphs.

Wow! What a thrill that was! Life immediately changed for both of us. We were on the same page again.

Cliff told me that it had happened a month earlier. He withheld it from me until he got home because he wanted to be with me and be able to rejoice with me when I first got the news. He knew how happy I would be.

I rejoiced regarding how God had answered all the prayers of the many people who had prayed with me for him for the past fifteen years; how God had proved once again, even to Cliff, who had a problem with this very issue, that he does answer prayer.

Cliff now once again understood that God answers every prayer of a believer; but like a good Father, sometimes he answers with a yes, sometimes with a no, sometimes with a not now, later, and finally, sometimes with a never, that would not be good, or it would not be according to my plan. I am so grateful that God reclarified these things in Cliff's thinking when he said, "Okay, I will believe." All of this made that day in 1979 one of the best days of my life.

After his faith returned, he apologized to the kids, too, for his actions. I am so glad that in spite of it all, they love their dad and now have a good relationship with him.

As a footnote, Cliff believes that one of the things that his experience shows is that people who believe in God and in the truth of God's Word can nonetheless block out faith in him and consciousness of him; and their condition can become similar to what he experienced simply by neglecting reading his Word and depending more and more solely on reason.

The many cassette tapes Cliff recorded during his research needed to be transcribed. I spent hour after hour in the months to come playing those tapes and typing what was on them. I was, however, glad to do it because it was through this endeavor that God brought Cliff back to the Lord.

46

Greater Involvement

With Cliff's return to faith and fellowship with God, the late 1979/1980 period of time represented a turning point spiritually in both Cliff's and my life. He began identifying himself publicly as a Christian and participating in Christian efforts both on and off of the university campus. This new development lifted both of our spirits. We were both again seeking to please the Lord. It felt so good.

While Cliff was very happy that he had returned to faith in God and his Word, he, at the same time, experienced a lot of regret about his past, regret about the years he had "wasted," the years when his views and demeanor had sent the wrong message to others—especially to his children and his students. He often could not hold back the tears when he shared his experience with others. A verse of an old hymn really struck a deep acute emotional chord within him. It expressed how distressed he felt about having been so unfaithful to God and others when it could have been so different. It went like this:

> Oh the years of sinning wasted,
> Could I but recall them now.
> I would give them all to Jesus.
> To His will I'd gladly bow.

One of the consequences of this sorrow over those spiritually "squandered" years was an intense desire to make up—with God's help—for those "lost years."

One of the ways Cliff began to do this was by declaring on the first day of his classes that he was a Christian and believer in the truth and authority of God's Word. He did this by talking about theories of causation in history. He talked about economic, political, social, etc., causes of history, and finally about the possibility of there also being divine supernatural causes of history. Cliff then told the students that he believed in the latter kind of causation also because he believed what the Bible says about causation and why he believed that.

Some students loved his readiness to be transparent about this and to give God the credit they also believed he is due; others were puzzled. Some were not ready to accept the idea, but none of them were downright ugly in their rejection of his position.

News of Cliff having "become religious" gradually spread throughout his department and the university community. He openly identified himself with Christian student endeavors on campus. For several years, he helped lead the effort to have Christian administrators, faculty, and staff sign the declaration, stating, "Christ is risen; He is risen indeed." It was published at Easter time in the student newspaper. Later, at a university-wide banquet celebrating the successful establishment of the university's archives, Cliff was asked to say grace.

Shortly after his retirement in 2003, Cliff mounted the effort to challenge the Theory of Evolution on campus by inviting Phillip Johnson, author of the book *Darwin on Trial* to campus. Johnson did a couple of public lectures which were followed by question-and-answer sessions. He also did a classroom lecture including a Q&A session as well as a lecture on public TV.

Prior to this, Cliff had also identified with other anti-evolution speakers who had been brought to campus at earlier times.

At church, Cliff and I were invited to join a group who saw spiritual things somewhat differently and who frequently socialized together. Some of them were involved in a prison ministry at the maximum-security Marquette Branch Prison. They invited us to join them. I wasn't anxious to be a part of that initially, but Cliff joined and went every Tuesday evening. The outside group that met at the prison were volunteers from various churches. They were allowed to meet in a large room with a group of twenty to thirty prisoners known as "trustees" under law enforcement surveillance.

It was a lively group. Many had come to love Jesus. They would form a large circle, and while standing and facing each other, they engaged in lusty singing interspersed with testimonies and prayer. The sessions ended with a Bible study around tables. Not all of them, however, were what they appeared to be.

One of these prisoners who seemed to be a very sincere Christian was up for parole. The volunteers had come to think highly of him. He could be released sooner if he could find a family who would house him for a few months. The leaders of the volunteers approached us about doing so, but I resisted. Eventually, with some uneasiness, I gave in and agreed to have him come to live with us.

He was quite a helper and very congenial; but then one day, he revealed to me that he had out-of-body experiences. He said that if I knew what he could experience, I would kick him out. That made me very uneasy. I wondered if he would wander into our bedroom?

He came to our place in about September and attended church with us. In November, he asked us if he could invite his girlfriend to stay with us for a few days. They were going to be married in a couple of weeks. Well, I said okay. She arrived from California in a white rabbit fur coat. She was different. She never lifted a finger to help with a meal or anything. *Strange*, I thought.

Their wedding date was approaching. I had planned to invite that volunteer group that went out to the prison to a wedding reception for them. But then one night, around the dinner table, the groom announced to us, "You are not invited to the wedding! I am a warlock, and my fiancée is a witch!"

We didn't know what to do. I went to the pastor, but he was of no help. We couldn't see the wedding happen fast enough and for them to be out of our house. This was just before Christmas. They had no money, but somehow, they got an apartment, and we learned where it was. I still had a little space in my heart for them. We couldn't invite them in for Christmas dinner with the family! So we took a turkey to them. We went up an outside staircase and knocked on the door. After a long wait, he opened the door, half-dressed, and gruffly said, "When you come to my house, call before you come! And, furthermore, this isn't the right entrance. Go down the stairs and come up the inside entrance!"

We were dumbfounded! We could have just stepped in from where we were. However, we obeyed and brought the turkey up to him in the way he wished! That was our last encounter with him.

Later, another prisoner was in the same situation, and we were again approached; but a parole officer came by and virtually begged us not to accept him into our home. He had been a sex offender. *Oops!*

Later, I joined Cliff in his visits to the prison. Some prisoners that we befriended were released from prison and became solid community members. For instance, one developed a successful tree trimming business, another was an accountant, and another became involved in Christian ministry. We continued our friendship with these guys after they were released; however, two of them have now passed away, and we have lost track of the other one.

Also, in the early and mid-eighties, with the children now gone and with Cliff more on board with me spiritually, I became more involved at church too. I was on the church's session and on a search committee for a new pastor. Interestingly, that new pastor asked me to be the master of ceremonies for his installation service.

Under his leadership, however, I didn't refrain from expressing my position on doctrinal matters with which I disagreed and about which I felt I should not be silent. For example, while I was on the session, a Sunday school teacher asked us if she could give communion to very young children. After all, she claimed, they had been baptized and, therefore, were children of God. I resisted this and sent a letter to the session, stating why I was resistant, also saying that I felt the Bible taught we become a child of God by faith alone, not by baptism. In the letter, I also stated that we should have a study of baptism. To quote, I wrote, "I move that we begin a study of baptism."

The pastor read my letter to the session, and when he read that sentence, he said, "'And I nominate Eleanor as the chairperson." That resulted in two years of weekly committee meetings, researching, and discussing the subject. I wrote a twenty-page single-spaced paper on it. Toward the end of the two years, a vote was taken as to which position the members of the committee held. All voted against the position I held, although one member said that he believed that the position that Eleanor presented was correct. Then he stated that for the sake of unity, however, he would vote with the majority against it.

The pastor stated that he wished the results of both reports be brought to the full session. He said that since Eleanor's view was widely held in Christendom, he wanted me to report my position as well.

For me, that was an intimidating challenge. I made a flip chart listing my major points. It was decided that the side of the majority report would present their views first. To give their report, their presenter basically dropped a pile of books on the table and said, "This is it." Basically, he was implying that the position of the majority had already been well-studied and reported on in the past; therefore, there was no need for him to prepare a further report.

I, in turn, gave a twenty-minute presentation. I began by saying this was one of the hardest things I had ever done—to publicly take a position contrary to what the pastor believed. At the end of my presentation, the pastor complimented me on my work and gave me a big hug, as did two others. Interestingly, even though my point of view was not adopted, the decision, at least at that time, was not to allow small children to take communion.

47

The Last Straw for Us

During our last year at that church, I participated in a seminar that was called the Stephens Ministry. After being trained in it to be a counselor, we were assigned a client. The group would then meet weekly to share our experience and possibly get some help in meeting any needs that arose. I had a client who had just lost her husband and shared with me that she didn't believe in an afterlife. She had a master's degree and was an avid reader. She would read anything I gave her. The pastor asked me, "How can we help you?"

I said, "Pray for her."

One lady in the group responded, "I don't think that's proper. She might be asked to do something she doesn't want to do."

With hands on my hips and in a firm upright position, I said, "Is it wrong to pray for someone? I think God has had a lot of experience with that. I think he knows how to handle that."

I did attend the next group meeting, and I apologized for my demeanor but not for what I said.

I told my husband about my experience. He said, "Well, that's the end of attending this church for me."

By this time, 1987, it had been eight years since Cliff's faith had been restored. What the Bible said had become more important than ever to him. He had become more and more concerned that our doctrinal positions lined up more precisely with what the Bible taught.

We began looking for another church. It was not easy to make the break. We had so many good friends in that church, such fine people in so many ways. Many of them had a very difficult time understanding why we were leaving the church after, especially me, having been so active and a part of it for twenty years. We tried to help them understand, but at times, it was very difficult.

48

A Great Accomplishment

Meanwhile, in 1982, Cliff experienced another switch in his academic responsibilities. He was asked by his department to establish an archive for the university. The objective was to develop a first-class archive that would not only preserve the university's own records professionally but also the records of at least the central portion of the Upper Peninsula (UP) of Michigan. He has written a book (327 pages on eight-and-a-half-by-eleven-inch-sized paper) on how the effort began and developed, so I won't repeat that here. Suffice it to say, he began the endeavor with little in the way of official administration support. The university had gotten along just fine without an archive so far. The thinking seemed to be, why did it need an archive now when there were so many other important places to spend the money?

Virtually, the only financial support Cliff received initially was the little that his department could muster out of its own regular budget. He began with only a nine-by-twelve-foot office and with no help. On the other hand, it was with a whole lot of moral support from his department. At times, he was granted one-third or two-thirds release time from his regular teaching duties. The administration did agree to that.

From this humble beginning, by 1993, Cliff, with full support from the administration, established a first-class archive at NMU based on fundamental archival principles.

Cliff in the Archive

That included the funding of a professionally-trained archivist who could take the archive onto the next level technically. That has made it possible to become the cutting-edge archive which it is today. It is now visited by people from many parts of the world. Many of its most important records are now digitized or scheduled to be. It has just now, in 2021, obtained a $100,000 grant with which to help digitize the most important records of many of the small-town communities in the UP.

Because of the foundation Cliff built to make this possible, the NMU Archive, or at least the current archivist, now refers to him with considerable pride as "The Father of the Archives." For this to have happened, it took an approximately six-year effort of promoting the need for a university archive and then another four to obtain agreements as to the kind of commitments that would be made for the archive to become the kind of meaningful preserver and dispenser of the historical source materials in the UP that it has become.

William Vandament, who was the president of the university during the final phase of this effort, had a lot to do with its final successful conclusion. Cliff and I greatly appreciated his insightfulness and helpfulness. He expressed his appreciation to Cliff for his efforts to make it happen. When it was all over, he sent Cliff a note, saying, "We couldn't have done it without you."

While Cliff was busy working with getting the university committed to having an archive, with his meager resources, he also was busy going as far as he could with the development of an actual archive. That is, he collected and processed archival materials. One of the consequences of this was the securing of the papers of the famed Michigan Supreme Court Justice and author, John Voekler. When Cliff, as archivist, heard that his papers had become available, he immediately took action to obtain them. Other archives also were very interested in acquiring them. His prompt action, along with President Vandament's strong support, secured them for Northern.

Cliff contacted Mrs. Voelker and personally helped retrieve many of the papers from her home himself. Judge Voelker, you may know, was the author of a best-selling book, *Anatomy of a Murder*. It was regarding a famed murder trial in the UP and was later made into a movie that is now world-renowned featuring the beloved actor, Jimmy Stewart.

Cliff's contribution to this 1982–1993 archival effort is one of the reasons the university hosted a university-wide celebration of this achievement in 1993 and is why he also was awarded the standing "Professor Emeritus" upon his retirement that year. Incidentally, he had also been awarded full professorship back in 1981.

I would like to finish this chapter on Cliff's establishment of an archive at NMU with a couple of quotes from the "Foreword" in his book that was published about 2015. Marcus Robyns, the current archivist, wrote:

> Cliff Maier committed his body and soul to
> the project of an archive for NMU with dogged
> and self-less determination.... This study has

solidified and enhanced my sense of awe, admiration, and appreciation for Cliff and his legacy.

I also wrote a foreword for his book after I typed it. In part, I wrote:

> I am amazed at the obstacles he encountered and endured to pursue his goal—now a fulfilled dream—of seeing Northern have an archive.... I can only say that my admiration for him has spiraled; it shows what can be accomplished in spite of great odds when a clear goal is pursued with determination and sincerity.

49

Some Special Happenings

Meanwhile, Mark's company, Chicago Research and Trade (CRT), had transferred him to London, England, in 1992. While there, he met his future wife, Tracey Fox. She was the Cash Manager at CRT, but not for long! Mark being stationed in Europe motivated us to take a trip to visit him while there and see some of Europe.

We consulted our travel agency to be sure we had all the paperwork that we needed to travel throughout Europe. We purchased Eurail Passes which allowed us to get on and off of trains wherever we wished. We used large backpacks to carry our necessities so we wouldn't have to check in our baggage and then wait to retrieve it when we decided to get off of a train. That also eliminated the possibility of lost luggage. It was the sort of thing the young folks did. So why not us too? I was sixty-four by this time, and Cliff was almost sixty.

We spent a month visiting England, Scotland, and various western European countries. One of my favorite cities was Venice, Italy. Travelling around the city in its canals in gondolas was so peaceful. We stayed there a couple more days than we had initially planned.

Venice

The most terrifying experience was when we attempted to visit Prague toward the end of our trip. We got onto the train in Czechoslovakia. After the train had already taken off, the conductor came by and asked us for our visas.

We said, "Passport?" We didn't have a visa.

He repeated, "Visa." That was the only word he seemed to know in English.

We responded, "Passport?"

Then he grabbed our passports, dropped them into a little box hanging around his neck, and walked away. When the train made its first stop, he escorted us into a small room with glass walls and a glass door. The glass was so dirty you could hardly see through it. He said nothing to us, locked the door, and left with our passports!

Momentarily, two guards came by and entered an adjoining glass cubicle. It was only large enough to hold a desk and two chairs. They said nothing to us, sat down in the chairs, put their feet up onto the desk, and it seemed like they fell asleep. There we were, no one was around that spoke English, and nothing was said to us! Our locked room had only badly worn-out armchairs, no bathroom facilities, no water, and no food.

I was terrified. Cliff seemed to be able to keep his cool. I wondered what they were going to do to us. Would we be put in jail or some other kind of detention facility? How long would no one come by to let us know what was going to happen? Would we ever get our passports back? The whole experience reminded us of stories we had heard of how things were sometimes managed under Communist regimes.

Finally, about four hours later, a man who could speak English came by and said that a train was coming and we would be able to return back out of Czechoslovakia where we would be able to obtain visas that would allow us back into Czechoslovakia to visit. He also gave us back our passports! Because of lack of time, we abandoned the idea of going to Prague and proceeded on our trip through northern Germany—West and East Berlin, some of West Germany—and on to England.

We had given no thought when we made our reservations with our travel agency in Marquette about needing to identify our citizenship. We were still Canadians. Czechoslovakia had a quarrel with Canada at the time. As a consequence, Canadians had to have a visa to enter the Czech Republic as the northern part of the country was known by this time.

Incidentally, we did finally become American citizens on June 21, 2006. Part of why we delayed doing it for so long was for sentimental reasons but also because it was quite a process. It took us two years to complete.

We can learn so many life lessons from things that happen to us. For example, when we attempted to visit Prague, we thought we had the right documents. Our substitute—the passport—would not do. We find that when we visit people and talk about what they think the entrance requirements are to get to heaven, they often respond that they have done good things and are a good person. Unfortunately, they will find, as we did, that the wrong thing will not permit a person to enter. The right document, if you will, for entrance into heaven is faith in Jesus and trust in the pardon he has provided for us.

The result, according to the Bible, of not trusting in the right thing will have such severe and eternal consequences.

We didn't get to all the places—including Prague—we had hoped to that year. But then Mark surprised us with a special delightful announcement. He would be getting married the following August in England. Would we come to his wedding? What a delight! We decided to go a month early to travel throughout eastern Europe this time. And we got a visa—just in case!

On our second tour of Europe, the most heart-wrenching experience was our visit to Auschwitz. En route there, a young man befriended us. He shared story after story with us. His entire family of over one-hundred relatives died in the gas chambers. When we were about to get on a bus, he pushed himself in front of us and sat down on a seat right behind the driver. I thought, *How rude.* When I got into the bus and was beside him, he stood up and gave me the seat. I felt badly about my judgmental attitude toward him.

When we got to Auschwitz, he put on his dark glasses and disappeared. I think it just must have been so overwhelming for him to think of all his relatives who had been put to death there. I could relay a lot of interesting stories about our trips to Europe, but I must not.

We concluded our trip just in time for the wedding. The wedding was held in a quaint historic church which was absolutely lovely.

It was in Brixworth in Northampton, north of London. The bride's father and stepmother had a huge beautiful historic home with a picturesque courtyard and garden. In it, they had set up an elegant tent with large windows.

It was lined with white cloth and had chandeliers hanging inside of it.

Tracey and Mark

It was a wedding you just don't forget.

Several of Mark's US friends joined us to be with Mark and Tracey for their special day.

Mark and Tracey's wedding and my family:
Cliff, Larry, Fern, me and Virgil

Mark and Tracey have given us two wonderful grandchildren, Jack and Emma. Both of them have loved sports and have excelled in them.

Jack and Emma

Emma was the catcher on traveling high school softball teams and made the varsity team as a freshman! Jack has played several sports. But unlike any one on my side of the family, while in high school, he also was a main feature in Show Choir, a travelling singing and dance competition team. I am so proud of and delighted with these two special grandchildren.

That same year in 1993, the university offered a buyout. We analyzed our finances. We had no debts. We decided we were set well enough for twenty years. We didn't expect to live any longer than that, if that long. So Cliff took the buyout. Now it is twenty-eight years later, and unless something drastically changes for the worst, we think we are still okay financially for another few years. Thank you, Lord.

When Cliff retired, he still had a huge academic project to complete. That is, the book about the Two Rivers Bible Institute. Work on it had been put on hold during the ten years while Cliff was working on the archives. TRBI, by that time, was named the Nipawin Bible Institute and would be celebrating its sixtieth anniversary in 1994. The hope was that the book would be completed for that occasion.

Working on the book had to be put on hold again. Right after we returned from our trip to Europe, we learned that Esther, Cliff's sister's breast cancer had taken a serious turn for the worse. Although they lived in faraway Saskatchewan, we just had to go and do whatever we could to help. We found Esther was pretty much already too weak to do much. I did much of the cooking and housekeeping while Cliff helped Dennis to get his crop off during this unusually difficult time. Fern flew in from California to be with her beloved aunt one last time. We stayed for three weeks.

Leaving her was such a heart-wrenching experience. We all knew that this was the last time we would see Esther alive. And she did too. Her last words to us were, "This is the last time you will see me." It was the last time—on this earth. She was a strong believer, and we knew we would meet again where there will be no parting. She died on December 3, 1993. Cliff drove back for the funeral to honor his sister and support her lovely family.

So far as Cliff's other siblings are concerned, his two full-blooded ones, Don and Betty, have also had heartbreaking struggles. Don, now eighty-six, lost his wife, Dorothy, due to cancer almost twenty-one years ago. Betty lost her husband due to a brain aneurysm in 2017. She still helps her sons on the farm. Both are in reasonably good health for their ages.

A couple of Cliff's half brothers and sisters have had severe health challenges. All of them have been successful in their vocations.

Of Cliff's two step brothers and sister, George was mentally challenged and died of natural causes at age eighty. Tragically, Alex died of suicide at age seventeen, and Diena disappeared in midlife without a trace.

Cliff's father died in 1977 of colon cancer at age seventy-two. He dearly loved his children and grandchildren and would do anything to bring them together for family events. Given his desire to live and enjoy his family, he wondered why he had to die so young! On this side of heaven, we'll never know the answer to some of these questions. Cliff says that his death played a role in his return to the Lord.

At his dad's funeral, the thought struck Cliff, wouldn't he look foolish if it turned out that what his dad and siblings believed was right and that he was wrong in what he had come to believe? It was a thought he couldn't shake; and from hindsight, it appears to have caused him to begin to reconsider his position.

When I think of Cliff's siblings, I am amazed at how productive and even formally educated, in some cases, they became. Three of his sisters—Esther, Betty, and Freda—were nurses. His brother, Fred, became a medical doctor, and Cliff obtained a PhD and became a professor. Two siblings, Don and Ruth, worked in industrial fields. David and Edwin became very successful grain and livestock farmers. All of them except Esther, of course, have now retired and are enjoying a peaceful happy life in Canada.

To think that the people I have just mentioned were the immediate descendants of immigrants who were pioneers and eked out an existence on a very small farm continues to amaze me. Initially, Cliff's dad believed that grade eight was an adequate education for his children. All of these achievements are, I think, very remarkable.

Getting back to writing the book, we did not get much work done on it in 1993. After that, except for bare essentials, we both spent our full time for seven months working on what became known by our family as "the book." It was a massive challenge. The book, entitled *A Journey of Faith: The NBI story*, was published in Marquette in the summer of 1994 in two volumes and is 700 pages long. Just prior to that anniversary, we hauled them in a U-Haul trailer to the school in Canada.

When we finished the book, I stacked up the manuscripts written by both of us and typed and retyped by me. The stack measured eight feet high! I don't wonder why my daughter intentionally flunked a mandatory typing class—her only D- ever in her life! She did not ever want to become a typist after witnessing all the typing that I did! It's interesting that the typewriter played such a large role in my life; Fern made sure that it would not in hers! Without that skill, however, this account would not have been produced either.

The sixty-year TRBI/NBI anniversary celebration was amazing. Many of our old friends from our TRBI days were there. The Wannops, who had treated me like family, were there. The Schroeders, who planned and arranged our wedding, were there as well. It was a very special reunion for us.

During our lifetime, we have done a considerable amount of traveling. We have gone on two cruises in the Caribbean. We have

Cliff and me at dinner on a cruise

toured much of the United States and Canada. For our fiftieth wedding anniversary, our children treated us to a week-long vacation in Riviera Maya near Cancun, Mexico, with the whole family present.

Grandchildren celebrating our fiftieth in Mexico

Before COVID-19, we made regular trips to San Jose, Naperville, and Appleton to visit our children. We loved spending time with them in their beautiful homes. Mark and Tracy have shown us many tourist attractions in the Chicago area. Fern and Larry have taken us to places like Yosemite National Park, San Francisco, Lake Tahoe, and more. They have also invited us to join them in their time-share in Cabo, Mexico. We accepted that invitation and spent a week with them in that lovely spot of God's awesome creation.

Beginning with the COVID-19 restrictions of 2020 and with our older age, one of the things we are enjoying the most now is just sitting on our backyard deck and watching nature. We especially enjoy watching the birds and the graceful white-tailed deer which pass through our backyard quite regularly.

Fern and me fighting COVID-19

We enjoy the beautiful setting that God has given us right here in our own backyard. I often think of the prayer I prayed on that rock behind our house.

A peaceful evening in our yard

50

The Years at the Tab

By the time Cliff retired in 1993, we had already been attending the Marquette Gospel Tabernacle (Tab) for six years. We would be attending it until 2000. These would indeed again be very busy years.

When we left the Presbyterian Church in 1987, we began our search for a new church by looking first at the doctrinal statements of the various evangelical churches of our area. We paid particular attention to what their position was on baptism. We were surprised to discover that one that looked very promising believed that baptism was necessary to complete a person's salvation. Another church believed "without holiness, no person can get to heaven."

A pastor of that denomination told us that if a person had even one unconfessed sin at the time of their death, they would not make heaven. It seemed that the position of at least some of the people associated with that church was that, ultimately, a person had to be holy on their own merits in order to enter into heaven. Yet the Bible clearly teaches that we are justified by faith alone in what Christ has done for us, not on the basis of our own merits or by baptism.

As we searched, we found that Bethel Baptist Church's doctrinal position was right in line with what we had come to believe the Bible teaches. We visited there, but there were only a handful of people present, and most of them were sitting at the far back of the church. It didn't look very alive.

Eventually, we felt that our best option was the Marquette Gospel Tabernacle. Their doctrine, for the most part, seemed sound to us, and it looked very alive. Their pastor, at the time, was a graduate of Bethel Seminary, a Baptist seminary in St. Paul, Minnesota. We did have a problem with a few aspects of their doctrine of speaking in tongues. They stated that whether or not a person did it, that had nothing to do with one's salvation. So we decided to attend that church.

By this time, Cliff had become just as involved in church and church activities as I was. From this point on, we began using our property to serve the Lord as I promised God we would on that rock before we had our land.

To get to know the congregation, we began inviting a good number of them to our house for dinner, family by family. We found a lot of very committed people and quickly made some great friends.

The church had an evangelism ministry called Evangelism Explosion (EE) that also included a great visitation program. As we were getting involved, the pastor sent us to visit a couple, Jeff and Jill Santti, who had visited the church. They recommitted their lives to the Lord that night.

Jeff said, "We used to go to bars on Friday nights. What do we do now?"

I said, "Would you like to come to our house for a Bible study?"

That was the beginning of a Bible study that lasted for years. Two other couples joined us as well. They were Eric Smith and his wife, Susan Syria, and John and Carol Redders. Eventually, some college students also came. That led to the creation of a college group which grew to quite a number. It lasted for at least as long as we were at that church.

The couples mentioned above have become special friends. We have kept in close touch, especially with Eric and Susan since they, too, now attend Bethel, the church we have attended since 2000. Their two sons, Jordan and Adam, became like our own two sons. In fact, the boys called Cliff "Papa" as they were growing up. Eric and Susan have been sort of on-call friends with regard to any special needs that have arisen for us—Jeff too. Over the years, Eric has helped us with some electrical changes in our house and has gotten us set up in the whole Internet service and has continued to upgrade it.

Susan edited and set up our first book for the publishers and helped edit this one. When Jordan recently proposed to his girlfriend, he called us to tell us. We were so pleased. Jordan's brother, Adam, during his high school years at Bethel, was a great joy to everyone including us. Today, both of these young men are advanced professionals. Jordan is an attorney and Adam is a business analyst/computer programmer.

Jeff and Jill Santti too have continued to be good friends. Their children, too, were like a son and daughter. When we celebrated our fiftieth wedding anniversary, Jeff told us he wanted to help with it and did.

For the opening of school at the university, we would throw a "Welcome back" party for students. A couple of times, we had a pig roast for the occasion. About eighty kids showed up. The church's youth pastor, Tom Colner, was great at organizing games and activities for the group and was a great spiritual leader. Jeff Santti and a few others, too, helped us to prepare for these events. We invited Tom to bring the church's youth to our house for various activities, and he often did.

Backtracking a bit, the senior pastor who had been teaching the evangelism seminar resigned about a year after we arrived, and there now was no one to keep it going. One day, we went out to dinner with Jeff and Jill. We were commenting about the fact that we would love to see that evangelism ministry continue. I said that I would be interested in going for the training but didn't want to go alone. Jill piped up, "I'll go with you!"

We contacted the church leadership about our desire, and they enthusiastically agreed to sponsor us. The training was in Florida. They even paid part of our way.

When we returned, I immediately started our first group session. That was the beginning of what would become an almost thirty-year involvement of teaching and doing evangelism. It became my/our life. We loved seeing people change from being timid about sharing their faith to becoming confident about doing it and obeying Jesus's great commission to share the good news of the Gospel with everyone—the world, as the Bible puts it.

John, one of our participants in the class, was having difficulty with his roommate who was suffering from Tourettes. He shared his experiences with me several times, and finally, I said, "Would you like to come and live with us?" Momentarily, he couldn't believe the offer, but then he moved right in that very night!

The next morning, however, we had not only John in the house but also another fellow by the name of Ed. His car, packed with all of his belongings, was in our driveway. He was one of John's roommates and had been experiencing the same difficulties as John had. Initially, we agreed to let him stay with us for a week. However, he seemed like a very congenial sort of guy. He was a new Christian who John had just led to the Lord as a result of being in the evangelism class. He had a big drinking problem. He said he drank seventy-four cans of beer a week. It quickly became evident that Ed needed help with becoming established as a Christian. So we invited him to stay with us also. Those empty bedrooms our kids had moved out of came in very handy again.

Since this was for a very good cause, we allowed them to stay with us, gratis. John stayed for a year and Ed for three years while they were both in school. John became a faithful pastor; and in the years thereafter, Ed became a fine Christian social worker who helped many troubled individuals both spiritually and socially. Ed also helped a number of his family members to become believers in Jesus Christ. We couldn't help but be thankful that we had the pleasure of playing a small part in their becoming mature Christians.

Since those two guys lived with us, we have had eight more students live with us. It has been almost continuously up to the present times, sometimes one at a time, sometimes two, and almost always gratis. Presently, for the past three years, a recent graduate of NMU, Keston Roberts, has been living with us. He is from Trinidad. Initially, we fed these students as well as provided them with a room in return for a minimal amount of help. More recently, I have felt that I no longer wished to cook for them. They, however, are free to use the kitchen after we are finished using it.

Returning to the late 1980s and 1990s, because of new obligations he took on, Cliff dropped out of the prison ministry. I, on the other hand, began teaching the same evangelism seminar that I was doing in church to those guys at the prison. Seventy-year-old Millie Greenwald joined me. The prisoners loved it. To demonstrate Gospel presentations, we invited them to bring other prisoners that possibly weren't Christians yet, and we would do a Gospel presentation for them. I can remember how one particular prisoner, when he heard that Jesus had died for our sins and that he could be forgiven, sprung up from his seat and then, falling to his knees, cried out to God to forgive him and told God that he believed in him.

Another prisoner that was transferred to a different prison began teaching the course to prisoners there. He wrote and told me of some of the success he had in teaching others to witness and of how some had come to love Jesus there too.

Millie and I did this there for three years until the administration needed our time slot for something else. It was interesting; one time, the chaplain came to our class to observe what we were doing. He listened to the Gospel presentation, and after we were done, he said that he felt like praying to accept Jesus all over again. He really supported our efforts. The prison even purchased the EE literature kits for the prisoners (I believe the kits cost about $30 at that time).

While we were at the Tab, I was on the committee that invited the Billy Graham Crusade people to come to Marquette. That event was led by Franklin Graham. Both Cliff and I were involved with canvassing the city, inviting people to come, and with counseling at the end of the meetings. A couple of very dear friends of ours made decisions for Christ.

Meanwhile, Cliff became involved in a task that seemed almost full-time. The size of the church building and its lack of off-street parking were recognized as factors that would prevent it from much further growth and from being a church that appealed much to college students. It was decided more space for building expansion and off-street parking needed to be created on the block on which the tab was located. This could be done by purchasing as many of the existing properties on that block as possible. Then the church would rent at least some of them for as long as necessary and eventually move or demolish them.

The idea was accepted, and Cliff became the main person managing the effort. After all, he was now retired and had the time, and he was enthusiastic about the plan. In a relatively short time, the church owned four new properties. We rented all of them. Three additional houses were already owned by the church and utilized primarily as a parsonage, church office building, and classroom space. Taking care of all of these properties, including their maintenance and repair, etc., took a lot of time. Thankfully, some members of the church stepped up and readily helped whenever they could. They became some of Cliff's best friends. They included people like Fred, Glenn, Chuck, Eric, Rob, Russell, and Pete. When Cliff and I left to join another church, some of them followed us, but not because we encouraged any of them to do so, except in one special case.

He and I also helped with the upkeep of the main church building and with recruiting help to do all of this. I have a photo of both Cliff and I on ladders, painting under the eaves at the back of the church building.

I often questioned Cliff's total commitment to his work on whatever he did. I even accused him of being a perfectionist and workaholic. I think he was to some extent.

My observation of Cliff is that when he does anything, he spares no effort to try and do it right. There is nothing slipshod about him. It doesn't matter whether it's gardening, painting, repairing things, working on volunteer projects, and I have to add teaching or creating an archive—it has to be done right.

During these years, Cliff was also concerned about helping with worthy community efforts. Hopefully, doing that would, at the same time, also create a positive image of Christianity in the community. Just before his retirement in 1992, because of his work on the university's archive, a couple of the members of the Marquette Maritime Museum recruited him to help upgrade the archival aspects of the museum. As time went on, because of insufficient volunteer or paid help to carry through on this goal, he arranged to have Northern's archives take on that responsibility.

Cliff found that other things around the museum also required a lot of upgrading—the appearance of the grounds and outside artifacts, the building's appearance, the internal exhibits area, the store and the storage areas, etc. He eventually became president of the museum's board.

While on the board, Cliff participated in a decision to build an addition to the museum to house an exhibit honoring the heroism of a Marquette native, WWII Submarine Captain David McClintock. Cliff participated in the creation and maintenance of an outdoor replica of his submarine and in the maintenance and upgrading of aspects of the indoor exhibits. When he left the museum in 2001 after being heavily involved with it for eight years, the board awarded him its most prestigious award, the "Ancient Mariner Award," for his contributions to the museum. The inscription on the plaque he received reads:

> In recognition of his many outstanding contributions to the museum in development and ongoing operations.

That year also, mainly because of his contributions to the museum, we think, the Marquette Rotary Club named him as one of four individuals it selected for its "Marquette Citizens of the Year" award.

In the late 1990s, the pastor at the Tab became ill but remained on despite the fact that he could no longer perform his duties satisfactorily. People began to leave. Opportunities to do ministry were waning. We revisited Bethel and found that the church was now full. There was life there, and it was exciting. While it broke our hearts to leave our good friends that remained at the Tab, we decided that a transition to Bethel would be the right thing to do for us.

51

Another Shocker

In 1998, I got some very sad news. My niece, Judy, called me from Prince Albert, Saskatchewan. She immediately said that if I wanted to see her mom and my sister, Frieda, alive, I needed to come right away. Hearing this was probably the biggest shock of my life. We arranged things in Marquette to be able to be gone for a while and arrived there in about three days. Fern also joined us to be with her cousins and aunt.

Frieda looked awful and was bedridden, except for brief periods of time. Judy arranged our visits with Frieda so each of us could have an alone time with her. Frieda shared with me that she was sure of going to heaven. I remember her telling me that the first thing she would do when she got to heaven was look for Mom. She also said that she was sure that her children were all believers and would meet her in heaven someday.

My sister had been a healthy person all of her life. She had just retired at the end of June, a little over a month before this. About two weeks after her retirement, she was diagnosed with very advanced cancer. By the middle of August, she was gone. Her five children came home and had no hope of seeing their mom ever recovering. Judy, Dan, and I were with her when she breathed her last breath. I said, "Frieda, the angels are coming for you." Tears flowed down our faces. I called her pastor who had been away on vacation. He was totally shocked, too, and came right over. He was just dumbfounded that this could be true.

Frieda and I were sort of like moms to each other, having been orphaned and raised by our aunt (Granny). I looked up to her; and she to me. I had hoped that we could be together more since she had

Me and sister Frieda—best friends

retired, maybe go on some trips together and just appreciate each other. It took me two years to not shed tears when I would think of her, and even as I write this, my eyes are full of tears.

She had so much to look forward to in her retirement years: five lovely children, nine grandchildren, and now six great-grandchildren.

Her children—Dan, Judy, Marilyn, Fred, and Patti—are all married and have all done very well. Dan and Judy are already retired and living a very peaceful and happy life in British Columbia.

Dan, Judy, and Patricia have their master's degrees. Dan married his bride, also a Marilyn. She is a retired pharmacist, and they have two wonderful daughters who have adorable children. One lives in Australia, and the other in Alberta. Dan achieved top positions in supporting and managing the government of the province of Alberta.

Judy married Jim Sellers in 1990. Jim has a masters of arts degree in geography, and Judy has a master's degree in social work. Jim has taught at Kwantlen College in British Columbia and has worked in senior level positions for both the governments of Saskatchewan and

Marilyn, Frieda, Patti, Fred, Judy, and Dan

the Northwest Territories. Judy has worked in social program planning and administration at the municipal, provincial, territorial, and federal levels and retired from the City of Vancouver as assistant general manager, Community Services.

Marilyn is married to Robert Evans and lives close to Lintlaw, my hometown. Marilyn has her bachelor's degree and is an author of many educational works.

Fred married Shauna (Penner) in 1990. He has his Journeyman's carpenter certification and has worked in a variety of carpentry positions in British Columbia and Saskatchewan. Shauna has a bachelor's degree in agriculture and has worked in different positions across western Canada.

Patricia Bader-Johnston and Brad have four grown children— Cohl, Taylor, Nicholas, and Maia—all of whom are pursuing professional training and careers. Patricia and her husband along with their youngest child still live in Japan. Their three older children returned to Canada for their higher education. The three of them, Frieda's grandchildren, just this year in 2021 all earned their master's degrees. Their grandma would have been thrilled to celebrate those accomplishments. Patricia was in corporate leadership positions in Japan and now is a successful entrepreneur. Brad is a music teacher.

Both Judy and Marilyn have and love their stepchildren. Both of them kept Bader as their last names.

Again, I have to say how amazed I have been when I consider the success and accomplishments of Frieda's children. Like Cliff's family, though different, they, too, had a difficult time in their childhood by losing their dad at such early ages. Yet they all have propelled to success in spite of it all.

About two years before Frieda died, my brother, Alfred, also died suddenly of a heart attack. He left his estate to his five siblings and named Frieda as the executor of his will. When she realized she would not be able to complete the task, she turned it over to her son, Dan. However, Dan was so broken over his mother's sudden death that he wanted me to help him handle it. I made two trips to his home in Edmonton, Alberta, to help sort through the material so he could finalize the whole matter.

A few years later, another brother, Otto, also died. Just prior to his death, my youngest brother, Hansie, called me to say that Otto is expected to have only two weeks to live. I was concerned about his spiritual welfare too. I had talked to him about it before, but he wasn't very receptive. So I hopped onto a plane and flew to Kelowna, British Columbia, to possibly have one last chat with him about his eternal destiny. Sadly, he wouldn't hear of it. I said that the Bible says, "We will bow to Jesus either here or when we stand before him."

He angrily responded, "I will bow to no one."

He lived a few more months, and I called him several times. He seemed to warm up to me some. I truly hope that he reconsidered what he said to me and is in heaven.

Of the eleven of us, only my youngest brother, Hansie, and I are still here. He had five children. One was killed in a horrible work accident. We have always lived so far apart, so I have only gotten to know Laurie and Connie of his children. Hansie is now eighty-nine and is bedridden in a nursing home. Thankfully, he says he believes in Jesus.

52

More "Retirement" Years

We were now in our seventies, eighties, and nineties. That should be "rocking chair time," right? It didn't turn out that way for us. The last twenty years of our lives have been happy, filled with lots of activity, and have been very fulfilling.

Cliff and me in our eighties

When we began attending Bethel, Cliff and I quickly felt at home. We were now fully on the same page doctrinally with each other and our church. Perhaps, like never before, we felt like we could pour ourselves into its goals.

On our first Sunday there, one of Bethel's most outgoing members, Mary Treml, invited us out for lunch with her husband, Pete, and one other couple new to Bethel, Dave and Alma Thomas. This was such a great first step in helping us to feel at home "right off the bat." It was also a great object lesson for us to emulate.

During the first year we attended, I sort of coasted, but we became members and looked into ways that we might serve. Cliff, though, almost immediately found some manual work that could be done around the church. Some friends, Fred and Lelia (Lee) Betway, who had followed Cliff and I to Bethel from the Tab, joined him. A plaque the three of them received from the trustees tells some of the story (we believe Mary Treml likely wrote it). In part, it states:

> The Trustee Board is so grateful for all the work that you did at the church recently. They (the board) are, to put it mildly, astounded!!! We are in awe of how quickly you availed yourself to pitching in and working toward…making the building a more delightful place.
>
> You have encouraged many at church with your willingness to use your talents and to get involved in our church…. The hours that you put in at the church painting, clearing out, and putting back all the many materials in the closet is really quite unbelievable…. May you have many more years in His service.

Except for leading the effort in 2005–2006 to redesign and refurbish the basement of a house Bethel purchased for its youth ministries, Cliff became heavily involved mainly with outreach rather than manual labor from 2001 to 2013.

During the summer of 2001, he went on a medical mission trip to Haiti. When he saw the poverty there and that a Christian school had virtually no adequate desks or equipment, he decided to do something about it.

At the time, some schools in the Marquette area were closing and were initially seeking to sell their surplus desks and equipment, but they were not selling. Cliff expressed an interest in them for Haiti, and from time to time over the next two years, a few school districts gave him a total of three railroad container loads of desks and equipment at no cost. Some members of Bethel and of the Tab did yeoman work in helping to collect and prepare the materials for shipment. To name just the most involved, they included Norman and Hilda Ball, Pastor Hank Steede, Dave Thomas, Bob Ray, Fred Betway, Bob Wilkinson, and John Janofski.

When Cliff returned to Haiti the following year, he was delighted to see the beaming appreciative faces of those children who were now sitting at much more adequate desks and reading from better blackboards, etc.

Cliff was elected to the Outreach Board in 2001. He assumed responsibility for organizing a Vacation Bible School for a settlement of Hispanic immigrants and their pastor in East Grand Forks, Minnesota. He did this for three or four years. Bethel's Outreach Board of the previous year had initiated that endeavor. As with the Haiti endeavor, this involved a good number of volunteers from Bethel and a couple of individuals from the Gospel Tab. In 2002, Cliff was named chairperson of the Outreach Board. That involved assuming primary responsibility for quite a number of additional concerns. I'll touch on them a bit more later.

I, too, was involved in some of the things Cliff was doing but was wishing that I could begin EE at Bethel. The wonderful experiences we had doing that ministry in the previous church had not left me. I had taught it there for nine years and for three at the prison. I shared some of what we did with some folks and eventually with Susan Michels, Chair of the Outreach Board at the time. She listened intently but didn't immediately invite me to do it. Eventually, however, she asked me to give it a try. I said that this isn't something you try for a short time. You really need a year to establish it and get trainers ready and available to train others. She agreed. I will enlarge on this later.

Meanwhile, during these years and throughout our retirement years, our secular life went on too, of course. For example, we experienced many happy times with our family.

Until about five years ago, we enjoyed participating in the various outings our children did when they came home for visits. One almost certain annual event was canoeing and/or kayaking down the Autrain River.

The last time Cliff and I went with them, we capsized our canoe—we say in order to provide the kids with some additional entertainment! Also that last time we went, I had a difficult time getting out of the canoe; that is, except for when we capsized it earlier! The kids joked that they might have to bring in a crane to have me lifted out of it! I finally made it out, but that was my last canoeing experience!

Family ready to go canoeing and kayaking

One of the things that is almost a ritual during many evenings when the kids are home is just sitting around our woodburning camp stove on our brick patio, visiting and reminiscing about past experiences, especially about things that were a little unusual or questionable, like, you know, taking the motorhome for a spin by a person only fourteen years old. In the evening, after dark, we especially enjoy the beautiful ambiance the floodlights create.

Family around the camp stove

Another favorite thing has been sitting on the beach and watching the grandchildren have fun in the water. Virgil has often also taken various members of the family on a cruise with his boat on Lake Superior or on a smaller warmer inland lake. The younger set, of course, enjoyed diving off of it or water skiing behind it, etc.

I have helped and watched with pleasure as our yard and garden has been developed, maintained and upgraded over the years. They are factors that have certainly provided much enjoyment not only for us but also for a good number of others who have visited us.

For example, in the last few years, we have organized an annual neighborhood "block party" in our backyard. All of us bring food to share. Our yard has a volleyball court as well as sufficient space for setting up two bocce ball courts.

Volley Ball court and rock garden wall
Cliff and Carol Anderson Becker in front

Bocce ball in our yard

After eating, some of us resort to playing a game. Others just continue conversing or watch the competition from the sidelines. Game-wise, we do pretty much the same thing at times when our children are home. It has been interesting to see the younger children pitch in and play with us older folks. We have a very special group of neighbors and have come to feel, in a sense (I think), like one big family. As people leave, if Cliff's garden has been productive enough, he has given them a vegetable or two. When the event is over, I have always felt good that we made another effort for us all to keep in touch and to get to know each other a little better.

Dinner inside with family

We have invited many people in for a meal. Often, the guests have been newcomers to our church. Sometimes I felt like I was a restaurant, but we both have loved it. In fact, when we were at the Tab, some ladies presented us with a patchwork quilt, thanking us for our hospitality. There are times, too, when we have gotten into discussions about spiritual matters, and sometimes some important decisions were made.

Until recently, we practically always had a weekly Bible study for college students in our home. It always included food. At times, some ladies from the church provided part of it. Sometimes we had parties for them—bonfires down by the creek, play volleyball, play indoor board games, etc.

Dinner down by our creek

Camp fire by our creek with family and friends

However, when we reached our eighties, we began to feel that it was time to pass on the baton. One day, out of the blue, Dr. Matthew Songer and his wife, Laura, expressed an interest in helping us lead the class. We not only agreed to let them help us, but we promptly turned it over to them. With food preparation and all, they then had the class at their home. Later, when the Songers became occupied elsewhere, Dr. Nathan Loewen and his wife, Brooke, took it over until COVID-19 struck (Nathan had participated in some of our events for students in earlier years). Each family always made great meals for the students, followed by a Bible study or just a discussion and a time of socializing.

We even were blessed with having two wedding receptions and two weddings in our backyard. One of the weddings was for Frank and Tristan Lombard; we introduced them to each other. This was the only time that we were matchmakers! They also were two of the students who had lived with us for a while. Both of them came from non-evangelical homes; today, they are pillars in an evangelical church. Things like this make me very thankful.

We have a wonderful church family too. So many are so very concerned when we have an issue. Many say to us, "Call me if you need something." They are so ready to help when we need it. An example is the good number of meals that were brought to us during my recent illnesses.

For a number of years now, we have invited our senior class at Bethel of about thirty people to our backyard for a summer picnic. They all bring their favorite dishes to share. The event is now led by one of our faithful members, Sandy Thomsen, who plans many events during the year for this group. I believe it was she who has dubbed ours "The Garden Party." She always plans some fun event. Recently, bocce ball courts were set up in our yard for the sports enthusiasts. Prior to Sandy's leadership, it was also led very effectively by Mary Treml, Jeanne Johnson, and Carolyn Deyo with the help of others.

In 2018, at one of our family meals on the deck, we celebrated Virgil's adoption of Karissa. She has been in our family for her whole life, and we loved that little girl.

Dinner outside with family: Virgil, Beth, Larry, Fern, Emma,
Tracey, Jack, two friends, Karissa, Mark, and me.

We have seen our three grandchildren grow up to be beautiful,
responsible people. None of them gave their parents a rough time
during their teenage years.

Cliff with his two sons and three Grandchildren

Jared and Karissa

Karissa has graduated from college and married Jared Buck in 2020.

Karissa's passion is helping children and young people become productive individuals. She has developed an organization to promote just that.

Part of Our new family; Jared, Tracey, Virg, Karissa, Fern, and Mark

Jack and Emma are now both in university and intend to pursue careers in aspects of the medical field.

They are all such delightful and responsible young people. We are so proud of each of them and love them so very much.

Emma and Jack, 2020

Virgil, after being single for about twenty years, found a great new wife, Beth Fisher, a high school friend. She is a retired ultrasound technologist. They went all out for their wedding in May 2018. The whole family joined them in Punta Cana in the Dominican Republic.

Virgil, Karissa, and Beth

Our Family: Jack, Fern, Tracey, Mark, Virgil, Beth,
Me, Jared, Karissa, Cliff, Larry, and Emma

Beth has a son, Brian, in college. We have just begun to get to know him.

Returning to our involvement at the church, in addition to the things mentioned above, Cliff and the outreach Board were, of course, primarily responsible for the church's relations with its foreign and homeland missionaries. This in itself involved a lot of different kinds of work.

The board was also focused on enlarging Bethel's ministry to the Marquette area. For a time, it brought in "big-name" speakers once or twice a year. In 2003, the board led in the effort to enter a float for the annual July 4 Marquette City parade.

The board also urged/supported local ministries to college students, Pregnancy Services, Habitat for Humanity, the Medical Access Coalition, Room at the Inn (a ministry to the homeless), Angel Tree (a ministry to children with a parent in prison), Operation Christmas Child and Compassion (ministries to needy children in foreign countries), the Salvation Army, and more. For a few years, quite a number of "Bethelites" volunteered to help Habitat for Humanity build houses for needy families. Cliff was one of the workers.

In 2010, Cliff was elected to the elder board and continued to serve on the outreach board as the elder board representative. Then in 2013, he stepped down from both of these boards because he had become too heavily involved with writing a history of NMU's archives and other things. He has, nonetheless, remained very active in the EE ministry as a trainer and in doing follow-up and hospitality-related types of things, etc.

I have been amazed how Cliff has thrown himself into the ministries of the church. As always, he put his whole heart and soul into whatever he did. I couldn't help but again praise God for restoring his faith. As he indicated, I think he felt like he needed to make up for lost time. His involvement, I think, also expresses his great thankfulness to God for bringing him back into fellowship with him.

By 2003, I was on the Christian Education Board (CE) and on a Pastoral Search Committee. That committee recommended that the church call Pastor Brian Oberg to be our pastor, which then happily happened. He firmly believes and teaches what the Bible says.

That has made Cliff and me happy. Pastor Oberg now feels led to step down next year (2022) after seventeen years at Bethel. I have been asked again to be a member on the next search committee. I pray that God will lead us to find his choice for Bethel.

As part of that CE board, I began a weekday Women's Bible Study. We organized child care, too, so that young moms could also participate. I led it for a couple of years and then, to involve others in the leadership role, asked Bethany Jentoft to take over. She did a great job and soon involved Abbie Tireman and others too.

The church's annual report for 2003 summarizes part of my involvement at that time:

> Eleanor Maier continues to volunteer her excellent organizational and recruitment skills to manage our adult Sunday School program and women's ministries. Her time and energy investment has resulted in prime educational offerings for maturing the faith of all attending.

I participated in planning the Vacation Bible School ministry before Becky Nelson became the Director of Children's Ministries.

There are other things Cliff and I participated in, too, but suffice it to say, we just enjoyed being involved in various ways. My/Our main niche at Bethel ultimately became doing the EE ministry until COVID-19 struck.

During these years, too, we usually took a month each year to visit our kids. Now, in June 2021, we are enjoying our backyard more than ever and are so happy that our family has just arrived, July 2, to enjoy it with us again.

Meanwhile, I have been working on this book for the last four months pretty steadily, and Cliff has been right in there with me. He was a great editor and actually wrote a few paragraphs here and there.

53

My Primary Focus

In 2001, I began to publicize EE at Bethel, and several people responded. Not only did we do it that year, but we continued doing a twelve-week seminar twice every year for the next nineteen years. During either the second or third year that we did it at Bethel, seventeen participated during the first semester and twenty-four during the second semester. Most semesters, the average number of new trainees numbered about five or six.

We have preferred to call the Evangelism Explosion program Everyday Evangelism (EE). We like to think of it as an evangelism and visitation ministry. Trainees were taught how to present the Gospel lovingly and convincingly. The inexperienced went on visits with the experienced trainers leading the way. When we first began EE at Bethel, we visited a lot of the regular attenders. We would ask them for permission to present the Gospel at their place so that the trainees could see it in action.

We also visited newcomers and visitors to our church when it seemed appropriate. People usually were delighted that Bethel was that interested in them to do that. Delighted, too, because by this time, very few pastors or their assistants were visiting their people in their homes. I remember how pleased one visitor was. He said that he had gone to church all his life and had never received a visit. Then he attended Bethel, and within two weeks, he got a visit. He was so impressed that he joined Bethel.

We did not go door-to-door for EE contacts. Eventually, one of the ways we obtained more contacts to visit was by participating in what NMU called Fall Fest. At it, various businesses and organizations could set up tables promoting their wares or services. We, as members of Bethel, also set up a table and attracted students by setting up dart boards for them to try their skill.

They were promised a free soda or bottle of water if they hit the target. Whether they hit it or not, they were given candy and their names were placed into a drawing for quite a nice sum of money. Before they were allowed to participate, however, they were asked to first fill out a questionnaire. Some questions were, "Are you sure of going to heaven? And would you like to know that for sure?" Another question asked if they would be open to a visit to discuss this. They just had to check boxes. EE teams would only visit those who checked the last question positively.

Me and Pastor Brian Oberg, ready for Fall Fest at NMU

We could always count on a good number of Bethelites to help with the setup, manning the table, and approaching students to ask them if they would complete the questionnaire.

Susan Michels wrote in a church bulletin that EE "is a tool that helps me share my faith. Not only have I seen that it helps me personally, but I have seen how EE has fanned the fire in our church to be more evangelistic."

Because EE has been a method of evangelism Bethel has used so successfully, I feel like I would like to give you an abbreviated and modified version of the presentation we share.

Important in it is to ask three questions after first asking for a person's permission to do so. The first question is whether or not they have come to the place in their spiritual life where they know for certain that they are going to heaven. Most people just hope so.

Then we tell them that the Bible tells us that we can know for sure and quote a verse in the Bible that says that. It is 1 John 5:13.

The purpose of the next question is really to once again ask for permission for us to go ahead with our conversation. We say, "Would you like me to share with you how I came to know for sure that I am going to heaven and how you can know it too?" I have yet to have someone say no to me.

Our next question is, "If you stood before God and he were to say to you, 'Why should I let you into my heaven?' what would you say?" We usually receive a variety of answers or guesses.

Then we share with them that the Bible says that heaven is a free gift. To get there, we just have to accept the gift. We tell them that the Bible says very clearly that we cannot earn our way to heaven. We cannot do anything to achieve it, except accept the gift God has provided for us to get there. We quote the Scriptures, Ephesians 2:8 and 9, that show that. We emphasize again that salvation—a welcome into heaven—is a gift. A person does not work for a gift, just accepts it.

Then we share with them that the Bible says in Romans 6:23 that we are all sinners. Most agree that no one is perfect and that we all sin at least some. We also tell them that it is our sins that stand in the way of us getting into heaven. Somehow, they must be deleted from our record. God, though he is loving, can't just wink at sin. His justice demands that it is dealt with. Then we tell them that the Bible also tells us that all of our sins are being recorded in God's record book or memory bank, if you will. I like to illustrate that by saying that it would be as if God had a huge mobile phone memory bank, and each time I sin, it gets entered into it. If I think a bad thought, in it goes, or say something unkind or do something unkind, there goes another entry into that record. I have often wondered how many times a day I sin. If I sinned only three times a day—once by what I said, once by what I thought, and once by what I did—that would be over 1,000 times a year! In my lifetime, that would add up to over 93,000 sins recorded in God's mobile phone memory bank for me.

We go on to emphasize that God is loving and doesn't want to punish us but that he is also just and must punish sin. So it looks like God has, or had, a dilemma on his hands. But he solved that by sending his Son, Jesus, to die—pay the penalty—for our sins and take our punishment for them, in effect to wipe them off of our record, if we accept his pardon.

We like to talk a little bit about who Jesus is as found in the Gospel of John, chapter 1:1–3 and verse 14. It says so much about Jesus in just these four verses. It says that he was God in the beginning and is God and also that he was the Creator of the world and of us. Then in verse fourteen, it says that he became flesh or was born a human. That's what we celebrate at Christmas. Many verses in the Bible state that Jesus came to earth, specifically to pay the penalty for our sins, to free us from that penalty. I like to refer to Isaiah 53:6 where it says that we are all like sheep who have gone astray, but the Lord (God) laid on Jesus the iniquity (our sin) of us all.

At this point in our presentation, I like to take my mobile phone and pass it from one hand to the other to show the transfer of the penalty of my sins from me to Jesus. The Bible says when we confess our sins and believe that Jesus is the Son of God who died to pay the penalty for our sins—in effect, accept the pardon Jesus/ God achieved for us—they are gone, forgiven. It is like God presses the delete button on his phone, and my sins disappear. "Isn't that wonderful news?" we say.

"Don't you agree?"

Now I tell the person that it is now up to him or her to decide whether or not they want to accept this awesome and wonderful gift of a life forever with God in a heaven that, according to the Bible, is so great that no one can begin to imagine what it will be like. We emphasize that they have to make this choice. No one, according to the Bible, can make it for them.

I like to end the conversation with a verse of scripture, John 3:36. It is a great promise or assurance and also an unmistakable warning. "He who believes in the Son has everlasting life; and he who does not believe the Son shall not see life, but the wrath of God abides [continues to abide] on him [because he or she has not accepted the pardon Jesus/God have made available to them]."

We leave them with a prayer that they can pray if they sincerely decide they want to accept God's free gift of salvation. It can be something like this, "Dear Jesus, I believe that you are the Son of God. I am sorry for my sin. I believe that you died to pay the penalty for it. I accept your pardon. Please forgive me. I gladly accept your gift of eternal life. Please help me out of gratitude to you to live a life that is pleasing to you. Amen."

We are always so delighted when someone accepts this great gift of eternal life that will spare them from a horrible eternity according to the Bible.

I am happy that I have witnessed a good number of people make that decision to accept Jesus's great gift of eternal life. There are several people in our congregation who have become committed Christians because of EE. It will be interesting and exciting when we get to heaven to see those who will be there because someone in EE shared the Gospel with them.

We are so happy that Bethel has allowed us to do this ministry. Pastors Bob Donaldson and Hank Steede were both supportive of it when we first arrived at Bethel in 2000. When Pastor Brian Oberg came in 2004, he immediately began helping to lead the effort. Some of the trainers who have been the most involved and great partners with us for many years include Dennis and Judy Caldwell, Gwen Timmons, Irmgard Miller, Irma Powers, Susan Michaels, Mary Treml, Mike Trenus until 2017, Millie Greenwald, Cliff, and, of course, Pastor Oberg as both a leader and trainer.

EE doesn't end with presentations and decisions that may have been made. To help a new Christian grow in their faith, we like to follow up with a visit and do Bible Studies with parties who are interested or free to attend and socializing with them and becoming their friends. As you may have guessed, my main ministry at Bethel has been doing EE, and I/we couldn't have been happier doing anything else, important as doing many other things are also.

54

Health Issues

As I look back on my life, I really thank the Lord for the generally good health he has blessed me with. In the last three years, though, I have had a couple of major issues.

In 2018, I suffered a severe stroke—a brain bleed. My face was twisted, I couldn't talk, and could hardly swallow. But thank God, in the first week, three doctors were already able to tell me that "my recovery was remarkable." I believe God healed me and used some excellent doctors to help with that. About three months after I had my stroke, I made a video and put it on YouTube. It briefly mentions my stroke and then discusses how we can receive God's greatest gift so we are ready to go when our turn comes. To date, it has had about 15,000 hits. At my age, I am pretty happy about that! If you wish, you can view it by going to YouTube and typing in Eleanor Maier Heaven.

Five months ago, I was suffering from a couple of threatening heart issues. The opening through my aortic valve, which should be about the size of a quarter in diameter, had decreased to be about the size of a pencil. I had difficulty breathing and had become discouragingly weak most of the time. One of my doctors recommended that I have the valve replaced. Another doctor told me that I had two weeks to two years to live. Another doctor told me they would prepare to send me to hospice. I struggled with going through with such a procedure at my age. One of my retired doctor friends advised against doing it. My family wanted me to have it done. The cardiologist we were considering to have do it had a high rate of success. I decided that if I did nothing, I would be dying soon, and if I had the surgery, there was a fairly good chance that I would live for some time yet.

So, with many people praying for me, I decided to go ahead with it. Following many preparatory tests, the doctors decided that I was a good candidate for a successful procedure. That is how it has turned out. I feel much better.

My pulse, however, was still very low, as low as thirty-five at times. The doctors recommended a pacemaker. Again, I struggled with going ahead with that but eventually did. I am sure that because of that and the valve replacement—and because of God's blessing—I have gradually regained my strength and now feel really good again. Thank you, Lord, and thank you, Doctors.

We are so thankful for our children. They are so good to us and they care for us with such concern when we are in need. For example, when I had my stroke, Fern spent three months with us. Mark came home for over a week, and Virgil, living in Marquette a lot of the time came when needed.

Fern, Virgil, and Mark

55

Reminiscing Once More

As I have reflected on my life, I can't help but marvel and be thankful for the way the Lord has guided and helped me/us through life and its many challenges; how he brought certain people into my life that made a huge difference on the road I travelled; how my mom got me started on my journey of faith by sending me to catechism; how my aunt took in us five kids and that she, too, was concerned about our spiritual development. Not incidentally, too, how that typewriter and that typing skill she launched me into has proved to be a great tool for my journey. Also, how she befriended the Quarks who taught me the way of salvation.

How Vivian Strickert, without her realizing it, influenced me to go to Bible school; how that decision in that raspberry patch further changed the road I have travelled; how Bible school impacted my life to live for God, and it was where my husband found me; how God brought us together.

How we were helped by many people during the tough years of our lives; how God blessed us with three wonderful children; how they have all become very competent successful individuals; how thankfully they all believe in Jesus despite our disconnect through which they lived.

How God brought my husband, Cliff, back to himself, more committed than ever; how that has changed the last forty years of our lives and resulted in the fulfillment of some of the hopes and dreams we had when we were dating.

How God has enabled us with the help of many trainers in the EE ministry to help others become believers and devoted followers of Christ and faithful witnesses.

How many prayers were answered on my/our behalf, not only during my physical illnesses during the last few years, but also throughout life. I am now wondering what God might still have for me to do, that is in addition to meeting him in heaven?

I can only say, "Thank you God for your love and faithfulness." With the hymn writer, I gratefully say, "*Great is thy faithfulness, Oh God, My Father. Great is thy faithfulness, Oh Lord unto me!*"

When I think of what I have just written about my/our past, I marvel at how God has brought things to my remembrance as if they just happened yesterday. It has caused me to think of what it might be like when I stand before the judgment seat of Christ and give an account of what I did with my life. The Bible says that we Christians will be required to do that (2 Corinthians 5:10). Our work will be tried, examined. Will it be found to be gold, silver, and precious stones, or wood, hay, and stubble? The latter of no lasting value, will be burned (1 Corinthians 3:12–15).

I know I have failed my Lord many times in my lifetime. I have wasted a lot of time too. My attitude and motives have not always been right either, but I also hope as the Lord examines my life, he will find some things of value—some gold, silver, or precious stones that he will be able to glean from what I did with my life. Sometimes it makes me wish I could have another shot at life.

The Bible also makes it very clear that those who have not accepted God's pardon will also stand before him. Sadly, the outcome, according to the Bible, will be absolutely horrible. If you happen to be one of those, please reconsider. Please go back and follow the steps outlined in chapter 53 of this account.

56

What's Next?

I don't know what's next. Heaven can't be far off. When I think of heaven, I get pretty excited.

When I think of seeing the God who created me with such a fantastic body with all of its marvelous features that function so beautifully together and also the God who created the awesome universe that he has allowed me to live in and to enjoy; and then when I think that this God loved me so much that he sent his Son to die for me so I could be saved from the consequences of my sins and be in heaven with him, I am overwhelmed. Also, to think that I will no longer have any more pain and will be in a glorified spiritual body—it's all too much to really grasp. The Bible says, "Eye has not seen, nor ear heard, nor has entered into the heart of man the things which God has prepared for those who love Him."

When I think of seeing God, the Father, and Jesus, there on their thrones in all of their glory with thousands and thousands of angels flying above them and with multitudes of people who have believed in Jesus gathered there in that awesomely beautiful place, I am overwhelmed. Like Fern once said, "It is too good to miss!"

Thinking about the fate of those who do not accept Jesus makes us want to continue to share with people how they can be sure of going to heaven. We want to help people understand that a choice and a decision must be made to enter the glories of heaven.

We would like to continue to be involved in our church's evangelism and visitation ministry, probably not in leadership roles but actively participating in some way. We would also still love to invite people to our home as we are able and make it available for church functions as well.

I/we, of course, look forward to what is going to happen in the lives of our children and grandchildren. The roads our grandchildren are taking look so promising for them.

I trust that this account of some of my/our ninety-three years of experiences, joys, struggles, and learnings might be a pleasure and a blessing and possibly even help guide someone on their journey in some good way. Please feel free to pass on the story and its reflections.

Remember that choices and decisions we make are vital. Decisions matter. Decisions we make will matter throughout all eternity. Let God be your guide. Proverbs 3:6 states, "In all thy ways acknowledge Him and He will direct your paths."

A good portion of my history has now been documented! Thank you for reading it, and may God bless you. I pray that God's will for you will be done in each of your lives.

About the Author

Eleanor graduated from Whitworth College, now university, with a bachelor's degree in Christian education. She has been active in church most of her life. Her husband, Cliff, graduated from the University of Washington with a doctorate degree in history and was a professor of history at Northern Michigan University in Marquette, Michigan, for twenty-five years. Between them, this is the third book they have collaborated on and authored.

They have been married for sixty-six years and have three grown children: Fern, George Virgil, and Mark; and three grandchildren: Jack, Emma, and Karissa. You can glean a character sketch of the author from the reading of this book. She was born into severe poverty and orphaned at an early age and was an introvert. By age twenty-two, she had become the administrative secretary and a teacher at the Two Rivers Bible Institute. She had graduated there from a four-year Bible-study program.

Throughout her life, she faced various and difficult challenges, even death three times. She experienced emotional, spiritual, financial, and family struggles. She and her husband's faith crises are among the most intriguing parts of her story. With God's help, she overcame them and has experienced many wonderful years. She gives God the glory for his loving care and faithfulness throughout her ninety-three eventful years.

CPSIA information can be obtained
at www.ICGtesting.com
Printed in the USA
JSHW031915060922
30037JS00001B/2